To —

Beulah Allison

with all good wishes

Hyman Judah Schuchtel

THE
REAL ENJOYMENT
OF LIVING

THE
REAL ENJOYMENT
OF LIVING

BY

HYMAN JUDAH SCHACHTEL

NEW YORK

E. P. DUTTON & CO., INC.

1954

Library of Congress Catalog Card Number: 54-9786

To

BERNARD AND ANN MOLLIE

Table of Contents

Preface

THE REAL ENJOYMENT of living is an art which we all would master. Here is an attempt to indicate how it can be done despite the tribulations of our era. This is not "escape" literature, nor that kind of verbal narcotic which, despite all the tragedy around us, foolishly proclaims that all is well with the world. For we live in a time of great trouble. Widespread is the fear of a totally destructive war, and everywhere men and women are profoundly dismayed because they are haunted by insecurity.

Neither is this a "theological" nor a "religious" book, in the sense that it deals with a particular doctrinal interpretation of salvation. It is not written especially for Jews, or Christians, or for Americans only, although the framework of reference in which it is written is obviously the Judeo-Christian tradition, as experienced by an American Rabbi.

This book is for all those who would rejoice in life, who would celebrate the happiness of being alive regardless of circumstances. Obviously, mental health and spiritual health are the primal needs of our age because modern man, for many reasons, is a maladjusted person. Clearly, there can be no true enjoyment of life if there is emptiness or conflict within. How to fill this emptiness with spiritual strength and how to resolve this conflict by reason and understanding are the objects of this volume.

Whoever desires a book which ridicules and belittles man had better not read any further. Whoever yawns in the

7

presence of beauty and sneers at the graciousness of brotherhood has no interest in these pages. But if you love life, or
want to love it; and if you are interested enough to follow
the thinking of at least one of the celebrants of life who
humbly believes that he might help his neighbor toward the
development of those healthy attitudes which are essential
for the enjoyment of living, then, you are invited to come
along.

This book could never have been written without the
exalting memories of my devout father, the brilliant guidance of my faithful mother, and the patient cooperation of
my devoted wife.

CHAPTER I

Making Life Worth Living

"MISTER, it's a dog-eat-dog world. When are you going to quit pouring out the sugary, sentimental, religious tripe about brotherly love, justice and peace! Wake up, mister, and see the dirt and the tragedy. See how they kick a fellow when he is down. How jealous they are of him, how they hate him when he stands up. Why talk of human dignity and decency when people are often so mean and destructive. Admit it, mister, admit it and say that life is a mess. It is not worth living."

This is what a man told me one day during a forum discussion. He was absolutely sincere. Moreover, many in the audience nodded approvingly during his remarks.

Surely even the most casual thinker among us is occasionally forced to ask himself the question, "Is life worth living?" The circumstances which prompt such a question are usually disturbing or frustrating. When we prosper, are healthy, when we are able to love and be loved, while we are earning a decent livelihood and enjoy our work, then we accept these benign conditions without question. Unhindered and fortunate, we have no urgent reason to probe into the meaning of life.

However, we make a complete turn about when our needs are not fulfilled and we come upon days of adversity. Afflicted with physical pain, weakened by illness and sickness, we are transformed into frantic philosophers who feverishly ask such questions as, "Why was I born—Why am I living—What is the use of it all?" Again, attacked by mental anguish, frustrated and disillusioned, we repeat with the ancient skeptic, "Vanity of vanities; all is vanity."

I believe this pattern of reaction holds true for most of us regardless of general cosmic conditions, but if you add to one's personal problems the profound fact of world-wide upheaval, it is not surprising to hear many of us exclaim, "This life is a terrible mess; it isn't worth living; it is, in essence, a tragedy."

But this is only one phase of the despair of our times. Consider the fast pace of modern living. Our pressures and tensions reveal their pitiful cost in the accelerating rate of death by heart attack and the living death of mental breakdown in ever increasing, appalling numbers. Thus, men die long before their time and leave their families without their guiding strength and devotion.

Our young sons leave home these days for the Armed Forces, and who can describe the aching hearts of parents as they wonder what time will bring forth? The other day someone said to me, "With all the awful things that are happening now, how can you expect people to believe in God, love, justice and in life being worth living?" I think that this comment is not unusual. Indeed, it is an integral part of the stormy state of affairs.

Let me go further with you. Come with me, in your imagination, on a visit to a children's hospital. Go into the rooms and observe how the little ones suffer. You see a baby tortured by illness, its face flushed with fever and crying piteously. You are overwhelmed. "How can the affliction of innocent children be justified?" you ask yourself. Then you see the children in isolated quarters who are ravaged by unknown diseases. You behold a father and mother weeping, for they have just been told that their child has died.

Why do I ask you to visualize these scenes of sorrow? Because we must not avoid any aspect of the misery and tragedy of our existence when we attempt to answer the question, "Is life worth living?" To be sure, we must also remember the happier side of our experiences, the recovery from illness, the beauty of the world in which we live, the great joys and delights that we know and the supreme blessing of all which is love. As Matthew Arnold said it, "We must see life steadily, and see it whole." Moreover, we should hearken to Spinoza's advice, and this I consider to be a most important concept, "We should view life under the aspect of eternity." By this Spinoza meant to say, as I see it, that every individual is an important, though small, part of the larger life of the world. We must regard ourselves as not only living in our own day but also as being the heirs of all the yesterdays and the progenitors of all the tomorrows. To quote Spinoza further: "At the same time, though I myself, body and mind, have a beginning and an end, in birth and death, nothing can destroy the fact of my existence. From all eternity, I am a part of history, one event in the infinite order and connection of events, which nothing can displace or replace, and to all eternity, I shall so remain."

We anticipate the essence of my answer to the question of whether or not life is worth living by stating that it is up to you and me to *make* life worth living. The happy life, the useful life, is not a gift. You are not going to win it as a prize, nor buy it like some piece of furniture. You, yourself, will have to make your life worth living. You will have to earn it. Struggle for it. Plan for it. The worthy and enjoyable life is the life which *you make* worthwhile. Similarly, the unhappy life, the wasted life, is usually due to what you have done to waste it and make it meaningless.

We cannot begin to calculate the amount of damage which is being done to people's lives by immature judgment which causes painful frustration and maladjustment. Take, for example, the plain, physical fact of being alive. From what most people say and do, you could conclude that they have forgotten there is such a thing as death. I am not introducing, I hope, a morbid note here when I remind you that we are born to die. We may die early, we may die late, but we will die. Shakespeare said, "We owe God a death." That we don't like to think of this doesn't make it less true. The ancient Egyptians were more realistic. They used to have a skull at their banquet tables, so that they might never forget, even at the height of their festivities and in the midst of their most voluptuous carousals, that death is man's unavoidable fate. Now once you assimilate this thought concerning death and its inevitability, you have the chance to adjust yourself to this reality. Running away from it, of course, can only lead to hysteria, and you eventually find yourself quite unprepared when death strikes—whether near to you or far. Accepting the fact that death must come, that it is the very nature of the human being to pass away, you may become humble and gentle and infinitely kinder to all those around you. You may then see yourself as a friend to others who are your companions during your sojourn upon this earth. Recognizing the physical limitations of life, you will be able to develop the faith and the courage and co-operation with others which are so essential in overcoming the difficulties and the trials of existence.

You will notice that I am stressing the importance of recognizing the basic nature of life. You have to know the facts. You must be aware of the quintessence of life. You must be able to establish, as a foundation for your philosophy, such truths as: we are born to die, we can lose our most precious possessions, we can suffer, we can know pain, we can fail, we can be disappointed, our dreams can be shattered, our hopes frustrated. Of course, this is only one side of the picture. The other side that we ought never to forget is that life can be happy, it can be excitingly beautiful and satisfying, it can bring the vigor of health, the thrill of achievement, the blessing of love, the supreme heights of aesthetic delight, from the appreciation of a sunset or a sunrise to the mysterious beauty of a little flower. Life offers its physical satisfactions and its spiritual joys. It can be wonderful to be alive, to think, to write, to create, to know friendship, to love children, to love people, to serve, to be of use, to help others. The important thing is that we develop an understanding of both sides of life, its joys and its sorrows, for only then can we have a balanced attitude and an abiding faith.

When will people wake up and realize that their immature conclusions and refusal to face facts, their evasion of realities, are major reasons for their failure to make life worth living? How long will it be before most of us understand that life doesn't owe you and me anything—not a thing. You may get from life only what you put into it. If you wait for your dreams to come true, without helping to make them come true, you will wait in vain. Long ago, it was said, "God helps those who help themselves." If you have lost a loved one, you are not going to do any good to anyone by remaining overcome with inconsolable grief. Remember the old adage, "Laugh and the world laughs with you, weep, and you weep alone." The human race has lived long enough to understand that the incessant weepers, and the constant moaners, are immature, and do not understand the true nature of life. Life requires strength, and gentleness, and humble resignation, and the laughter of faith and confidence.

The same philosophy holds true for all of life's burdens and difficulties. What if you have failed, or you have not obtained your fondest wish? You have no business moping and lamenting that the world is finished for you, that there is no hope for you. Every one of us fails sometime; every one of us falls down sometime; we all have tasted the bitterness of defeat. But that is not real failure. Real failure is when you don't try again; real failure is when you continue to lie there after you have fallen down. You must get up and try and try again. If a friend betrays you, or your husband or wife has failed you, or your children have been ungrateful, even so, these tragic experiences do not justify your concluding that all friendship is unreliable, that every marriage is a failure, that all children are ingrates. The only thing you can say is that, in your own particular experience, you have been disappointed, or unsuccessful.

Nevertheless, you may indulge the hope, quite justifiably, that next time it will not be as it was; that next time it will be better; that if certain conditions are corrected, the whole picture will change measurably. You will thus avoid the evil of extremism in your thinking and in your reaction to what life brings you. Being a realist, you cannot be disillusioned with life. Instead, you will be proud of your own responsibility toward making your life worth living. And what is most remarkable of all is that every one of us has the capacity to rise above all of life's pain and tribulation, if only we will make use of "inner power."

James Gilkey tells us, in his essay on man's heritage, that "There is hidden within each one of us a secret self which is ultimately invincible. No matter how heavy our burden, how perplexing our problems, how intense the strain circumstance throws upon us, that inner self never wholly gives way. Time and again, we catch glimpses of it—calm, poised, unafraid. It looks out at us from some secret window of the soul, like a strange, brave face gazing from the casement of an unexplored castle." We can agree with Mr. Gilkey, for we know that this invincible inner self has been developed through millions of years, during which the human race has experienced a constant struggle against tremendous obstacles and hardships. Slowly, our capacity for resistance and struggle and conquest has come to life within us, and it is there for you and me to use, if only we will reach down deep enough for it.

During two decades in the ministry, again and again I have been impressed with the ability of people to measure up to the demands of a major crisis. I have never forgotten my first service at a child's funeral. The parents said nothing to me. The few words that I spoke seemed to have been uttered in vain. They didn't appear to be listening. We went through the service at the funeral chapel and then came to the most trying moment of all, at the grave. As the little casket descended, I could see the eyes of the father and mother following that coffin to its final resting place. They were drawn to it by the magnet of their parental love—they were saying farewell to the most cherished, the most beautiful blessing they had ever known. I wondered if they would ever leave that sacred spot. The friends gathered there were silent, stunned by the abject melancholy of the agonized parents. Finally, I went up to the mother and said to her, very quietly, "It is time to go home. Your child is not in that coffin—your child is with God, and in your heart forever." She bowed her head, and taking hold of her husband's arm, they walked together, slowly, to their car. I remember praying silently then, "O Lord, Thou hast made us so strong. Thou hast given us the power which can provide us with the fortitude to carry the most exacting burdens of life. O Lord, I have just seen how these parents were able to turn away from the one spot in the world which contains the remnant of all their hopes and dreams; they turned back to life again. Though they will weep, though they will sorrow, yet will they continue to live. And perhaps, Thou wilt bless them with another child, with children. They will live again, and this tragedy which is so bitter now, will become a sweet memory—a dream of yester-year to enrich their lives evermore."

As I concluded, it seemed as though my meditation communicated itself to their wounded hearts because at that moment I saw their eyes lifted heavenward, illuminated with the light of hope and faith. This experience made me realize as never before how powerful is the inner resourcefulness of the human being as he meets and overcomes major disasters.

When we face reality and open our eyes to the truth, you and I know that the future belongs only to those who are courageous, who are spiritually strong, who refuse to be downed by the blows of life. Then let us rise up if we have fallen. Let us smile again if we have forgotten how to smile. Let us believe in God if we have run away from Him in our confusion. Remember, always, that behind the clouds, the sun is still shining; that beneath the snows and barrenness of winter is a soil which throbs with life. To keep on working and hoping and praying, regardless of the inevitable set-backs of existence because you refuse to say die; to do this is to have learned how to live. To do this is never to ask again, "Is life worth living?" For you will be among those blessed ones who are *making life worth living*.

To refuse to learn this truth, to shut our eyes to this reality is to make impossible the realization of that enjoyment in living which God grants to all who are willing to work for it. We permit ourselves, sometimes, to stand in the path of our own quest for happiness. Often you have said of another, "*He* is his own worst enemy." What about yourself? Do you prevent yourself from making your life worth living? Do you deny yourself the enjoyment of life?

CHAPTER II

The Enjoyment of Life

ONE AFTERNOON, as I started to drive on a busy, congested thoroughfare, I decided to turn up a quiet avenue where motoring would be more pleasant. Leisurely and easily, I drove on an undisturbed street and then on through the park, reaching my destination in a calm and relaxed mood.

Afterward, as I reflected upon this experience, I realized how important my choice was, and how meaningful it is when applied to life in general. What a pity it is that so many of us don't use the sense God gave us to come up for air, to avoid unnecessary complications, to take the time to enjoy life. Most of us are so involved in the business of making a living, are so strained, so nervous, so tense, that we forget the art of living. Following some kind of perverse logic, we cling to the crowded roads, the busy thoroughfares, forgetting that the charm and beauty and peace of life are found on the side roads, the byways, not on the highways. We crowd ourselves too much; we push ourselves too much and before we know it, we have forgotten how to enjoy life, how to be happy.

God has put us here to bring happiness to others and to find happiness in living. Our supreme objective is to build upon this earth one of the provinces of the Kingdom of Heaven. We are not going to do this by denying ourselves the opportunities to appreciate the world around us. We are not going to do this by driving ourselves into a neurotic state because of our neglect of hobbies, amateur interests, which have nothing directly to do with making more money, but which have everything to do with making for ourselves more happiness. One must admit that the issues which confront us in the business world and the political world are so vast and potent that it requires a struggle to keep from being overwhelmed by them. Nor am I suggesting that we should seek to escape from meeting these issues squarely—to the best of our capacities.

However, we shall not be able to deal intelligently with our lives unless we take time out to think of the inner man, the spirit, the soul. How long is it since you have gone out for a day in the country? How long is it since you have taken a long walk? Was it as far back as your childhood days that you recall the last time you lay on the grass and looked up into the skies, enchanted by the majestic clouds which, like the "stately Spanish Galleon coming from the Isthmus" of John Masefield, moved across the celestial ocean? When did you last gaze with rapturous attention at the stars and moon, the myriad twinkling eyes of the night? Is that, too, part of your remote memories? When have you walked through the Zoo, visited the Museum of Natural History, enjoyed the exhibitions of the Art museum? When was the last time that you opened the pages of a great novel, or read poetry, or listened to a symphony? The world of nature, the world of art, literature, and music, the pursuit of knowledge, these are primary sources of that enjoyment of life which can bring stability, serenity of soul, and tranquillity.

Perhaps you are saying, "Oh, it's easy for a minister to think like this because he has the time for it; or he has been trained for it; all that is a part of his life's work." But you are wrong. The life of the ministry is so involved with details that it is just as difficult for me, as it is for you, to find time away from the business of living to be able to experience the enjoyment of life. Everyone of us is pretty much in the same boat these days when it comes to being inundated by onerous duties. Whether you are a housewife, a factory worker, a truck driver, a teacher, a doctor, a lawyer, or whatnot, it is hard to adjust your schedule, your daily routine, to make room for other interests. And yet we must somehow find the way to break the chains which make us slaves to the demanding chores of life.

We seek escape and relaxation in many kinds of activities. Certainly, the American people are famous for their interest in baseball and football, popular music, radio, television and a host of other similar pastimes, not to overlook varied forms of gambling, from cards to races. Some of these types of amusement and relaxation are fairly good; some of them are harmful; few of them restore the soul; few of them contribute to inner peace and abiding satisfaction.

Children, just like grown-ups, usually are fidgety and out of harmony with any kind of hobby which calls for mental reflection. I have watched my own children and their friends and I have made comparisons with what I recall from childhood. When children get together these days they either go through an imitation of their favorite Western on television or in the movies, or else they are engaged in some other form of mock killing. I seldom see children playing marbles any more, or hopscotch, or hide-and-seek. They do very little reading. They are beginning to develop at a very young age the neurotic forms of behavior which they see in the adult world around them.

I don't recall that twenty-five or thirty years ago, little girls of ten, eleven and twelve wore evening dresses for their parties. Nor were boys wearing formal clothes at thirteen. I certainly don't remember little boys of five and six in long pants. Even childhood today is being speeded up, rushed—that childhood which ought to be a kingdom of the imagination, of charm and delight. Scarcely do our little ones begin to grow when they are aping the frenetic pace of their elders. Our children are sophisticated long before their time. Then, and this is perhaps the most disturbing observation of all, they are bored long before they should ever know what it means to be bored.

But our children are only reflections of their parents; they are carbon copies of the unhappy adult world; their standards, their goals, their interests are imitations, quite naturally, of what they see in their homes. Dr. Eric Fromm, a renowned psychiatrist, wrote recently that the greatest misfortune which could happen to most of us would be to find ourselves confined, alone, to our rooms for three days, with just enough food and books. He went on to say, "I think you would have thousands of nervous breakdowns after the first day." I agree with Dr. Fromm that most of us have lost the art of entertaining ourselves, of enjoying our own company. We have to dash out and be with other people, even though most of our social experiences are boring. "The bliss of solitude," to use Wordsworth's rewarding phrase, is something most of us have not developed and it is a state which most of us shun. We seem to be in conflict with ourselves, shaken by a constant trembling of our emotions. The result is that we eat faster, play faster, as though our lives depended upon hurry, rush and speed. Small wonder that heart attacks and mental breakdowns are commonplace. Small wonder that we so readily respond to the jingoist, the warmonger, the man on horseback, and are impatient with those who speak in the gentler terms of arbitration, discussion and peaceful settlement.

This was brought home most forcefully to me during a recent visit to Switzerland, a country which has enjoyed peace for six hundred years. The moment you enter that beautiful little land of soaring mountains and gracious valleys, heavenly lakes and charming cities and villages, you sense the presence of divine benediction. More impressive even than the grandeur of nature in Switzerland is the grandeur of its people, who, despite barriers of language and historic differences, blend together in amicable union. One night my wife and I went to see a Folk Festival in the lakeside city of Lucerne. First we were entertained by a series of folk dances which were simple and sweet and in some respects recall the square dances of our own country. This was followed by a chorus of twenty men who sang Swiss songs and featured yodeling. After this came the Alpine Horn blowing contest. And finally, there was a Flag Throwing exhibition, in which the contestant throws an emblem as high as he can into the air with the object of catching it by its standard, or pole, before it reaches the ground. Between these acts, a fine orchestra played some favorite Swiss folk music and that was the whole program.

I readily admit that it was tame compared to the exciting effect of a Spanish bull fight, a French duel, or an American boxing match. Indeed, one of our American friends there at the time scornfully declared that if this represents life in Switzerland, this calm, peaceful expression of Swiss folk ways, that he couldn't think of anything more boring in the world. And this was conclusive proof that peace, so far as mankind is concerned, is the mother of dullness, lethargy and stodginess. As I heard him say these things, I was reminded of a speech which Orson Welles delivered in that fascinating movie of some years back, called "The Third Man." Perhaps many of you saw the picture. If you did, then you may remember how Orson Welles, talking to a companion, speaks contemptuously of Switzerland. In general terms, he said something like this:

"Only war and struggle bring out the best in mankind. Only aggression, competition and conflict make for progress. Why, just look at Switzerland! Switzerland has known six hundred years of peace and what has it produced which is original in those six hundred years of peace? A coo-coo clock!" I can still hear the sneering, disdainful tone with which he pronounced the words, "coo-coo clock."

Well, I don't know how you feel about coo-coo clocks; I happen to like them very much. Indeed, we bought one of them over there and not only is it a good timepiece, but also it is delightful to have in the home and my children are intrigued and amused by that little bird which emerges on the half hour and the hour, and in the soft, musical, amusing notes of its species, announces the time.

I know very well that comparisons are odious, but I want to ask you this question: which do you think is better, at the end of centuries of progress, to produce the coo-coo clock or the atom bomb? As for me, I'll take the coo-coo clock which, I may add, is comparatively an insignificant product of Swiss industry, commerce and art. My fondest dream is to see the whole world enjoy the tempo and standard of living, the pleasant and fraternal way of living, which is to the glory and honor of the Swiss people.

It is high time that you and I, in our individual lives, call

a halt to the frantic pace we pursue and create in each day
an oasis, a Sabbath, a Switzerland, in which we find peace
and have the time to enjoy life. Perhaps you can find this
restoration of the soul in the development of true friendship, or maybe you can achieve this by reading from the
Bible, or listening to the inspired musical works of a
Beethoven, a Mozart or a Brahms, or by regular worship
in the House of God. Perhaps, most of all, it can be found
in taking the time to enjoy family living. Where else will
you discover more enduring blessings than those waiting
for you within the sanctuary of your own home? When a
husband and wife learn to know each other, to become two
people who enjoy each other's comradeship and partnership, they experience a happiness which is as balm to the
soul. And when parents take the time to know their children, to talk with them, to read to them, to guide and help
them, they know a thousand times the thrill of a gardener
who sows seeds in the good earth and tends the soil and
watches, with awe and gratitude, the growth of beautiful
flowers.

I happen to be one of seven children and as I think back
on the home in which I grew up, I remember my mother
and father doing something for us in those early years
which represents the chief blessing of my preparation for
adult life. My father, of blessed memory, who departed
from this earth much too young, and my beloved mother
who, thank God, is with us, contributed a powerful, wonderful strengthening conviction in the minds and hearts of
their children, which was this: that every child in our family knew that we, the children, came first before all other
considerations in the lives of our parents. We knew we
were loved in the real and most important sense of such

love. We came first and that meant more to us than anything else we enjoyed in our happy home.

Why don't you let first things come first? Isn't love a first thing? And faith and the growth of the mind and the spirit first things? Why continue to let second and third and fourth things come first? Of course, you must work hard and strive with all your capacity to make good in this world. But what does it profit a person to win a kingdom, if he loses his soul!

This life of ours, no matter how long it be in terms of time, is short compared with eternity. The years fly by as in a dream and almost before we know it our chance to do some good for others and for ourselves is gone. What a pity that we should forget, as one writer put it, that "life is too short to be little." How sad that all that we may be able to point to, at the divine judgment seat, is a life lost in the helter-skelter of meaningless, selfish existence. Your life is a gift from God: live it divinely, live it beautifully.

I once heard a man say he was most unhappy because of the emptiness of his life, even though he had much in worldly goods. I heard him say, "What have I after all these years of working hard? I am tired, I am bored and I feel as if I had one foot in the grave." And I said to him then, as I say to you now:

"Why must you continue to live at a pace so furious, in a routine so dull, without having developed your inner spiritual resources, without having discovered the real enjoyment of life? Why not live with your senses alert to beauty, with your mind enriched by the uplifting and saintly thoughts transmitted to us by the music and literature and Scripture of the gifted minds of the ages? Instead of living with one foot in the grave, why not live with one foot in Heaven? Instead of the weariness, the disillusionment and the tragedy of living out your days and years in a deadly, uninspired monotony, which stifles the soul and binds you to the earth, why don't you give yourself the chance which is yours for the taking, the chance to enjoy life: the chance to be what God meant you to be, not only the child of earth, but also, and which is far more important, the child of Heaven?"

CHAPTER III

The Normal Life

A MAJOR REASON for our failure to enjoy life is our mistaken idea of what is normal and abnormal and our erroneous concept of success and failure.

Let us consider the common complaint, that a normal life is impossible in our time. Now, whether or not the world is as irrational as it appears to be to some people, the fact remains that current affairs are definitely uncertain and insecure. Consequently, in such a period, it is not surprising to hear people sigh and long for the good old days. Furthermore, you may be sure that when people fear the present and glorify the past they will exaggerate the good of yesterday and magnify the evil which is at hand.

Why should people in our country today look back longingly on the past? Why should we be saying that our lives are abnormal and that the greatest blessing that could come to us would be to enjoy once again the so-called normal life of bygone days?

Granted that there is much to be shaken about in world affairs because of our struggle with Communism! Granted, too, that we have vast domestic, social and economic worries! Yet, despite these ominous conditions, our lives need not be abnormal.

For what is the normal life? What do you have in mind when you say that one thing is normal and that something else is abnormal? What are normal values and what are abnormal values? What constitutes the essential ingredients of "normalcy?" It might help us if we were to try to find some acceptable definition of the word "normal." A dictionary gives us the following: (1) standard, regular, natural; (2) occurring naturally; (3) belonging to the average in intelligence or development; (4) free from mental or nervous disorders; sane; mentally balanced.

These explanations of the dictionary are helpful and we may apply them to our subject by saying that the normal life is the life which is healthy, sane, balanced, organized, connected with reality and satisfying. Conversely, the abnormal life is the life which is sick, insane, unbalanced, disorganized, disconnected with reality and dissatisfying. Now, reducing these adjectives to one, if we may risk the danger of over-simplification, we might say that to the average person the meaning of the normal life is that it is a secure life which is happy, whereas the abnormal life is the insecure life which is unhappy.

Since, undeniably, there is so much insecurity and unhappiness today, we conclude that modern life is abnormal. But we must ask ourselves the question: "What is the essential cause of our unhappiness, our abnormality?" Part of the answer, I believe, is found under the general heading of false expectations and false standards of normalcy.

Let us apply one first question. One of the traditional rights of free men is the right to be different. In recent years this right is in danger of being destroyed. Most of us listen to and see the same programs on radio and television, and the same movies. We come to accept certain stereotypes as being normal and any deviation from them to be abnormal. For example, we expect to see all people wearing the same styles in clothing, the same styles in hair dress, having the same intonations in speech. Should a person not conform to these standards, he is immediately regarded to be queer, somebody strange, abnormal, a crackpot. Thus, we like to have people talk as we do and think as we do. We become uncomfortable in the presence of differences. We become even intolerant of differences.

The point cannot be overstressed that such intolerance runs counter to the *normal* standards of American liberty. Moreover, were intolerance to have prevailed in the early stages of our history we could never have reached our present power. For our nation is composed of many different types of people from all parts of the world. Tolerance made our country possible. Democracy comes alive precisely at the point where it is tolerant of differences. The moment that we insist upon everybody's using the same words, and thinking the same thoughts, and dressing in the same styles, and acting in the same manner, we no longer have a democracy but a totalitarian state cursed with the rigidity of regimentation.

Surely, you have heard of the New England Town Hall Meetings. At these meetings Americans met and proudly expressed themselves as they felt on all issues without fear of being regarded as abnormal or crackpot, because of not agreeing with the majority point of view.

Certainly, one of the greatest jurists who ever sat upon the bench of the United States Supreme Court was the late Oliver Wendell Holmes, Jr. Do you recall the title by which he is best remembered by those who honor him, and read of him, and rejoice in him? The Justice was known as "The Great Dissenter." Over and over he dissented, and differed with the majority of his colleagues on the bench. He often, together with the late Justice Brandeis, wrote minority opinions which are now regarded as classics and which, years later, came to form part of the logic of the majority opinion on other cases.

The point we make here, however, is that on the highest tribunal of our land, freedom of speech, freedom to differ, the freedom to think otherwise, is the normal pattern of behavior, which is respected, and expected. The same holds true for both houses of Congress. In the Senate, as in the House of Representatives, men rise up and differ with one another. Surely this should be, and must be, the normal practice of everyday American life for every American. Unless we want to lose our freedom, unless we would suffer the abnormal tyranny of Nazism and Communism, we must learn to respect differences, to consider it normal to speak out our point of view, even at the risk of displeasing whatever powers may be.

Patrick Henry once exclaimed, "Give me liberty, or give me death." That stirring, eloquent cry should still be heard by thoughtful Americans who would continue and preserve our free way of life. Unless we keep the right to differ, the right to express ourselves freely, the America we love will perish.

One must admit that it is not going to be easy to preserve the distinctive, normal American ideals of freedom in the atmosphere of insecurity and fear in which we live. And yet every American must strive with all his strength to keep from being overwhelmed by the pressure to conform, to think alike in every respect, to "keep up with the Joneses." At the same time, with the same amount of strength and fervor, we must teach ourselves and our children to affirm the great principles and uphold the laws of our American democracy. Surely we need to believe in and to accept with all our heart and soul the responsibili-

ties of freedom as expressed in the Constitution of the
United States and in the Declaration of Independence. We
must honor the dignity of every human being, and take
seriously our pledge to the flag which speaks of "One nation, indivisible, with liberty and justice for all." However,
to accept these wonderful principles is one thing; to develop false ideas of patriotism and distorted notions of
loyalty on the basis of these principles is another thing.

There is an additional phase to this discussion of the
normal life of people and the damage done by false expectations which should be explored here. We, the citizens
of this great country, are being misled by false expectations
and false standards of normalcy when we assume that there
must be no obstacles in our path, no challenge to meet, no
enemies to overcome, no dangers over which to triumph.
People rush to the conclusion that life is abnormal in
America today because there is military conflict and the
threat of a greater war. Yet, from the very beginning to
this hour, our nation has been involved in struggle with
every kind of threat to the security of American life. War,
conflict and dangers have more or less beset every generation of Americans. We have had wars early in our history,
with Indians, with France, England, Spain, and Mexico.
In modern times we have had war among ourselves, in
Europe, in Asia, all over the world. We have encountered
constant struggle with economic and social and religious
bigotries and barriers. We have been overwhelmed by
social and industrial revolution and all of us have been involved in our own personal struggles, even as every generation of Americans has striven against certain odds to
make its way in the world.

Why then, should we now be expecting that our national
life be different from what has been? What has led us to

the erroneous conclusion that our life is abnormal today because our nation is in peril?

Why, we have always been in peril! We have always had to remember the honored American watchword that "Eternal vigilance is the price of liberty." How false, then, are the expectations which anticipate a national life that is removed from all harm and danger, which can progress placidly and undeviatingly toward untroubled and calm destinations of ever increasing Utopia achievements! Yes, there has always been the American dream of a greater and finer and better future for all the people. But the dreamer has known, or should have known, that there is no magic Aladdin's lamp to rub, which can realize the dream effortlessly, suddenly, and completely. And, as vital as the dream has been to Americans, we have had in the past enough of realism in the majority of us to make us get down and work out painfully and sacrificially the outlines of the fulfillment of this dream. What kind of crafty seduction has woven a spell over our minds today which leads us to the false conclusion that the American dream can be achieved without pain, suffering, disappointment and sacrifice! Surely, we are naive children with undeveloped minds when we expect of our national life a sure and certain journey toward a majestic fulfillment.

It is time that every American citizen understands that freedom is not free, that "Americanism" is not something to be picked up at a bargain counter, that democracy cannot be had for the mere asking and taking. Indeed, we should know, and teach our children to know, that the American dream is constantly in peril and that no generation can be free from the obligations which were that of the very first generation of free Americans, to be ready to pledge life, fortune and sacred honor for the preservation and development of our American independence. True, the enemies of our democracy are more numerous today than ever before. Certainly the implements of war are the most fantastic and awful that have ever been devised. And the crisis is world-wide. Nevertheless, we do irreparable harm and injury to ourselves and our country when we fail to meet this enormous challenge with stout hearts and courageous spirits. Thus, the primary reason, it seems to me, why we deplore the national situation and cry aloud against what we call abnormalities is because of our false expectations and our faulty knowledge of American history.

In our personal lives, too, false expectations account, in large measure, for our widespread mental and nervous disorders. Consider the concept of success, as applied to our functions in life. We shall deal with this concept more extensively in the next chapter, but let us examine it briefly at this time. We seem to believe that we are misfits whenever we suffer failure in our personal efforts. When we are unsuccessful in a business venture we see in such failure the dreadful proof of our personal inadequacy and permanent incapacity to make good. We have become so hypnotized by the gospel of success that we have come to expect that in everything we do there must be a triumphant conclusion, that there cannot possibly be any disappointment. Whence comes this infantile distortion of the truth? On what basis and logic have we the right to conclude that if we try and fail, if we don't get the results we are after forthwith, if we do not succeed in some venture, that something must be wrong in us, and therefore wrong with the world? Have we forgotten that ancient definition of genius, which is, "The courage to make mistakes?"

All men, no matter how big, have made and do make mistakes. Henry Ford forgot to put a reverse gear in his

first automobile. Edison once spent over two million dollars
on an invention which proved to be worthless. The man
who makes no mistakes, who does not fail, lacks the bold-
ness of the spirit of adventure. It is well known that Babe
Ruth set the record for home runs but it is not common
knowledge that he was struck out more than any other
player. Similarly, we know that Ty Cobb stole more
bases successfully than anyone else but few recall that he
was also tagged out while stealing bases more than any
other man in baseball history. The truth then, you see,
about life is that men struggle and fight hard and make mistakes and fail on their road to success, whether they are
hitting a ball, building a business, or writing a symphony.
Moreover, you cannot succeed without failing at times.
It is normal to fail and to make mistakes; it is normal to
meet with defeat and be frustrated. What is abnormal is
to remain thwarted—to surrender when you strike out—
to give up the fight when you don't make good. The successful life is in large measure a matter of trial and error,
making mistakes, failing. It is a false evaluation of life
which insists that the theme of success is just one sweet
song, a constant, growing crescendo of triumphant music.

The tremendous extent of the havoc wrought by these
erroneous ideas of how to be successful is greatly increased
by our false standards of success. Suppose someone asked
you, "What is your standard for normal success in marriage, in business, in citizenship, in any phase of living?"
Would you say that success is making a lot of money, enjoying great reputation, being well known, being well
liked? What do you consider to be the most desirable
achievement in your business or profession, in your particular role in life? Is it to win widespread acclaim? What
would you say is the normal ambition of American youth?

Is it to be famous, a star athlete, a motion picture celebrity, a distinguished scientist, an honored statesman?

It is, of course, difficult to answer these questions when we consider the wide variety of goals toward which we aspire. But, skipping the argument, let me risk stating here that success to many of us seems to be the attainment of riches and the power it brings. Generation upon generation of Americans have been indoctrinated with this ambition. When I was a boy, the most popular books for juveniles were the Horatio Alger stories. The pat formula used in these books is the presentation of a poor boy who, through hard work, integrity and devotion, rises from rags to riches. Now there is nothing wrong in the goal of wanting to become economically and financially secure. This is a good objective and it has accounted in great measure for the remarkable materialistic advance of our mighty nation. But to say that the successful life is the wealthy life is to place an abnormal value upon financial achievement. A man can live the most successful life without coming remotely close to being rich in worldly goods.

Some of the most successful lives you and I know are not found in "Who's Who in America." We have found success among unheralded teachers, devoted mothers and fathers, humble clergymen who dedicated themselves to the good of others, obscure public servants who, in the course of their duty, whether as policemen or firemen, or plain laborers, were faithful to their jobs and were proud of doing their best in upholding the dignity of a community. Thus, it seems perfectly clear that what is supremely great and successful about our country is not defined by its material riches and growth, but by the number of its citizens who have given themselves in a spirit of dedication and love to family, to friends, to the greatest good of the community and nation. We do our children and ourselves a grave injustice by holding up to them as a symbol of success, as the norm of achievement, the accumulation of a large bank account. Please don't misunderstand. We are not charging that it is wrong to be financially successful and that it is evil to acquire riches. But it is wrong, and it is evil to teach another that unless this is done, and material goals are attained, that his life is abnormal and miserable and that he is a failure.

It is precisely because we teach such false doctrines that the extent of unhappiness and disillusionment and failure which has overcome people in our time is perhaps greater than ever before.

CHAPTER IV

The Successful Life

HAPPINESS IS not having what you want but wanting what you have.

Because most of us have not learned this truth, the easiest thing to find nowadays, it seems to me, is skepticism, cynicism and discontent. "Why aren't you happy?" I ask a young man. "You have the job you went after. I remember how you told me that if you had this job, you would be the luckiest human being alive. You were positive that once you obtained this appointment, the moment the contract was signed and you knew you had this position, then you would be happy. But lo and behold, you are not happy. You are miserable. You don't seem to get any joy out of your achievement."

And then I speak to a husband: "You told me that when you married this girl you would be the happiest of mortals. She was your dream girl. She was the answer to all your romantic expectations. How well I recall what you said when your first child was born. Why, you believed that to be a parent was to win honors higher than a king's. Your cup of joy would overflow. But, now you are not happy and you are troubled and you act as if life has turned you down. You don't get a thrill, any more, out of romance, out of being a parent."

We could describe many situations in which people at

one point in their lives seem to be certain that they will be successful if they achieve a coveted objective, and then later they derive no enjoyment from the fulfillment of the dream. We may conclude that one of our universal human failings is to permit anticipation to exceed realization. We seem to be profoundly excited while reaching for some goal or person, but once we get what we are after, we often change and we lose interest. Our excitement and happy feelings frequently fade after we get what we thought we desired and we lapse into a state of dismal boredom and life becomes a dull routine. And yet, realization does not have to be a disappointment. It doesn't seem to me that the aftermath of the attainment of the dream has to be disillusionment.

Let me submit what seems to be, according to my view of things, the major causes for our disillusionment, our boredom and sense of failure. Too many of us have that immature approach to life in which we are anxious to have things, to win romance, to enjoy privileges, but we are not willing to meet the responsibilities and the problems which go with these blessings.

Do you remember the excellent interpretation of the Cinderella Story by Walt Disney? What are the words that we see on the screen after Cinderella marries the Prince? They are the words which form the conclusion to most of the fairy tales. They are, "and they lived happily ever after." These words reveal that unrealistic approach to life which must lead to disappointment. We assume that all we have to do is to get married to the girl or man we think we love and we shall live happily ever after, as a matter of course. It is just going to happen of itself. We don't have to do anything about it. We work and we love and we build and we hope and we dream and live our

lives on the naive assumption that everything we undertake
to do must happen easily and beautifully and perfectly
without any extra effort on our part. We refuse to admit
that there can be such a thing as a challenge or a disappointment or a problem or a difficulty which we must
solve in the best way we can. And when the inevitable
problems arise we are disconsolate. We are like the little
girl who, not getting her way with her playmate, cries
out, "I'm going to pick up all my dolls and I'm going
home." However, not being able to pick up our dolls so
easily, when we are grown up, we sit around and sulk and
act embittered and spoil our relationships with people. We
get divorced, break friendships, give up jobs.

In my own ministry, I make it a point to talk things
over with a young couple about to be married. With such
a couple I never fail to stress the point that no matter how
much they think they are in love with each other and
how well they think they know each other, the realities of
marriage will surprise them. I say to them, "One of these
days you are going to say to yourself, 'Is this the man I
married?' or 'Is this the girl I married?' 'I had no idea he
was like that, or she was like that.' Never forget that
though you are Mr. and Mrs. you will still remain individuals with your own peculiarities, with your particular
greatness and your littleness. You will have to adjust to
one another. You will have to accommodate yourself not
to the strength so much as to the weakness of the other.
I want you to realize that the happy marriage is based upon
deliberate thought, hard work, careful planning, and,
above all, as the noted French writer André Maurois puts
it, 'The resolve to make your marriage a success.'"

And then I add, "I want you to know that the odds are
against you. There are very few people who use their in-

telligence and understanding to make a success out of marriage. You are going to face the danger of taking one another for granted. You are going to meet up with the problem of being upset by the other person's idiosyncrasies and weaknesses, pettiness, irritabilities. You will need all of your wisdom and will power, yes, and you will need all of your real love to surmount these obstacles. But, if you are wise enough, realistic enough and love each other enough, you can succeed."

One of the major faults which causes us to fail in life is our refusal to realize that the fulfillment of our dreams will demand from us a great deal of responsible action and thoughtful care; that realization of our hopes may bring problems which are most trying and difficult, that there can be unpleasantness ahead. If we want to live successfully, we had better become realists enough to admit that there can be numerous vexing problems, indeed, there will be much we must do in order to earn for ourselves the reward of real accomplishment and real attainment, whether it be in our marriage, in our work, in our profession, as a member of society, or whatever the case may be.

But this anticipation that life brings problems which we have to work out is not enough, unless we add to it the knowledge that it is the way of life and the nature of experience to be, very frequently, tragic and disillusioning. Why will man fill his days with anguish and his nights with tears, simply because he refuses to admit, what is so apparent all around him, the frequent tragedy in life, the sorrow and the pain, the untimely death, the friend who isn't true, the hopes which lie shattered in the dust? Why don't we see that life frustrates as often as it fulfills—

perhaps more often. That, where at times the world seems
to be a bed of roses, it is just as often a vale of tears.

Granted, it is difficult for most of us to see beyond our
own little private worlds. For example, if the weather is
warm here, it is hard for us to think of anyone freezing
elsewhere. Since our buildings remained intact here during
the war, it is hard to picture the destruction abroad; because we satisfy our hunger, we do not seem to realize
what starvation can mean. And yet, the truth is that every
night, the majority of the human race goes to bed hungry
and poorly clothed, in wretched dwellings that are unfit
for human habitation, enslaved by social, political and
economic bondage. Even when trouble or pain come very
close to us, we still can't seem to realize that we, too, are
profoundly involved. To be sure, we know what pain
means the moment our own tooth starts to ache, or we
find ourselves in the hospital facing an operation, or we
lose our job, or we find ourselves betrayed. And then,
shocked that this terrible thing could happen to us, we
collapse completely, we cry out that God has cheated us,
that the world is faithless, that all is ugliness and despair.

Frequently we hear people say, "What did *I* do to deserve such a fate? Why should this happen to *me*, of all
people?" It seems useless to say to such a blind person,
"But these things happen all the time. You have only just
become aware of them. Yesterday it was your brother.
Today it is you."

Now this sense of the frequency of life's disappointments
and pains, when properly understood, ought not to make
for a morbid outlook on life. On the contrary, it should
strengthen one for whatever may happen in life. With
the right understanding, you do not, when you are re-

jected, cry out that life has hurt you, *you* especially; or that life has cheated you, *you* of all people in the world. You will accept these things philosophically, calmly, for you will know that it is the way of life to try us at times to the utmost. And only when you comprehend these things can you be successful and the master of life.

William Henley, in a hospital the night before a serious operation to which the doctors resorted as the final desperate measure to save his life, did not write a lamentation. He did not say farewell to the world, he did not curse life, nor did he lose faith in it. Instead he wrote words which have been an inspiration to you and to me whenever we read them, whenever we think of them: "It matters not how straight the gate, how black with punishment the scroll; I am the master of my fate, I am the captain of my soul." After he recovered he called the poem "Invictus." Thus, he was the champion, the victor over his fears and the threat to his life because he met them with understanding, with courage, with resolute will.

I have known numbers of people who have stopped believing in God because their prayers were not answered, who look at the world without confidence, who see nothing but frustration everywhere because their wishes have not materialized. Whenever I can, I tell these people the story of a simple man in a town in Poland who expressed, one night, an attitude toward frustration and sorrow which is one of the greatest insights into the true nature of the successful life. This man was a pious soul who lived with his beloved daughter, a little ten-year-old. His wife and son had passed away and now all of his love was concentrated upon this child. Then one day his little girl became ill and the doctors told the father that the child was dying. Whereupon he announced that he would go that evening to the sanctuary and plead and argue with God. By nightfall the little synagogue was crowded and the people stood in awe as they watched him approach the Holy Ark, open it and cry out, "O Lord, I have come to appeal to your eternal righteousness and justice. I have always walked in Thy ways. I have never turned aside from the path of rectitude either to the right or to the left. I have done nothing but Thy will and have loved all my fellowmen." And then he turned to the congregation and exclaimed, "Is there anyone here whom I have wronged, intentionally or unintentionally?" The congregation exclaimed with one voice, "You have always been a saint in our eyes." He turned again to the Ark and declared, "O Lord, my daughter lies ill, at the point of death. She is my only one, the apple of my eye. You have taken my wife and my son, and now, must you also take my beloved child, my only one? Answer me, O God, answer me! Let not my just portion be withheld from me." At this moment a messenger approached and told him that his daughter had died. A terrible silence filled the sanctuary. The man bowed his head and, as if speaking out of the profound depths of his soul, he softly murmured these words, "This too is an answer, this too is an answer. Blessed be the righteous judge."

To reach such heights of understanding of life so that we can accept with faith whatever befalls us, graciously accepting our sorrows and disappointments, even as we are so ready to accept our joys as the blessings of heaven, is to be prepared for whatever life brings us. To reach this state of maturity of mind and spirit is to hear God even in the silences, to sense His presence in the darkness, even as we so readily perceive Him in the light.

Unfortunately, for so many of us, there is such a wide,

wide gap between our spiritual preparedness and the realities of experience. Most of us are childish, weak and ready to surrender all of our dreams whenever we stumble and fall, whenever what we ask for does not happen, whenever we don't get what we strive to attain. We refuse to meet our responsibilities. That is why so many of us are failures. We have a false standard of values and a false standard of success. We are superficial and too quick to relinquish our ideals at the first sign of disappointment. We won't work hard at earning and keeping our happiness. But the truth is that this life of ours is to be lived and to be lived gladly, intelligently and idealistically with a sense of humor and a sense of proportion and with reasonable expectations. But our ideals should be protected by a practical view of experience.

If I were to put it all in one paragraph, I would say it this way: This is the wisdom for the successful life—to work hard, but not to expect too much; to love but not to deem it inviolable; to dream but not to rage at the rude awakening; to believe in God but not to rebel and blaspheme if our prayers are unanswered; to live on as righteous men and women but not to deny the righteous life when the inevitable sorrows overtake us; to be gazing upward, ever upward with such eager intensity that the light of our own eyes lends color and radiance to the world around us, so that we can go forward undaunted and faithful, unafraid and confident, meeting successfully whatever betide. If it be skies of sunshine, to enjoy them deeply, knowing how unusually blessed we are. And if it be skies of clouds, to find even in the clouds the rainbow of promise.

It is when you possess this wisdom which bestows upon you a keen awareness of participation in life and grants you the dignity of "cosmic citizenship," that your life can be successful. However, it is impossible to win this precious victory as long as you refuse to let your mind conclude what the facts of life conclude. Such a refusal makes disillusionment inevitable—makes you come to believe that you have been cheated, that you are lost and that you are alone.

CHAPTER V

Supreme Partnership

To BELIEVE AND FEEL that one is alone is one of our greatest human tragedies. This sense of loneliness depresses the spirit and deprives a person of the capacity to enjoy life. In the last messages left behind by suicides, there is a single theme which runs through all of them and it is the poignant cry, "No one cares about me. I am alone."

To be tortured by this ravaging thought is to long for a final escape. The lonely heart is miserable and full of tears. It feels that it can beat in unison with nothing that life has to offer. It exclaims, "I have nothing left to live for, I am alone." A woman who lost her husband said to me, "Oh, I go out and see people. I try to keep busy. But when I come home at night, I cry myself to sleep, for when I come home, I am alone." A husband whose wife passed away, whose children have married, confessed to me, saying, "I spend my time trying to run away from my sense of loneliness. Only now, when my life's partner is gone, do I appreciate the profound meaning of the Bible's words, 'It is not good for man to be alone.'"

Surely we know, by this time, that gregariousness, the necessity to be with other people, is fundamental in all of us. To have friends; to enjoy companionship, to be recognized as a desirable member of a group or unit, is essential for the normal mental and physical health of an individual.

46

There is no greater punishment for a human being than to be placed in solitary confinement. We need one another; we depend upon one another and when this is denied to us we become physically and spiritually sick. Indeed, the first and surest sign of a mind that is breaking is when we see a person deliberately withdrawing from social contact and choosing to be a recluse, a hermit.

When a child of ours goes to school and doesn't make friends, when we find that he is alone, we know that we have a basic cause for worry. The essential ingredient of society is the sense of kinship, of togetherness, of belonging. Take that out of the human heart and mind and you have robbed the human being of his dignity and sublime responsibilities. Let me remind you that in a war we must first overcome the feeling of kinship with the people of the enemy nation before we can fight against them. We must first convince ourselves that our enemy is not part of the brotherhood of humanity; that he is beyond the pale of human worth; that he just doesn't belong to our way of life, before we can be roused in an organized effort to kill him. Thus, we come to hate the person or group about whom we have constructed the walls of our particular prejudice. In this example, you have the shocking evidence of our innate need for feeling a togetherness with other people if we are to live with them in brotherhood and peace. Wherever we turn we see that it is unhealthy for the individual, as it is dangerous for a nation, to become isolated, to become separated from the wider social group. It is not good for a person to be alone and it is not good for a nation to be alone.

However, we must learn that partnership and comradeship are not entirely confined to being with people. A person is not alone who is companioned by certain great

ideas. There is such a thing as finding abiding satisfaction
out of kinship with noble thoughts, cultural interests, and
spiritual ideals. If we use our minds, if we cultivate the
love of music and art and literature, the love of doing
good to others, the love for the supernal glories of nature,
one need not be alone. A major goal of life is to live in
such a manner that when we are physically alone, we
really are not alone.

It is important for us to stop and take stock of ourselves, in order to see wherein we are capable of main-
taining our balance and happiness even though alone. You
might well ask yourself the question, "Am I doing anything to nourish my spirit, my mind? Am I bored with
myself? Am I only making a living, or am I also learning
how to live?" Such a question, when used to probe
deep enough, can expose the truth about ourselves, which
is the first step necessary toward what Dr. Harry Emer-
son Fosdick calls, "victorious living." To see ourselves
as we really are is no simple matter. It is amazing to what
extent a person will go to deceive himself. One of the
major reasons for self-deception is wishful thinking. We
want to believe that whatever we are doing, we are doing
well. It pleases us to tell ourselves that we are doing our
best, are working hard, that we are leaving no stone unturned on the path of making our life as significant as
possible. Moreover, we refuse to believe that we are failing as a parent, as a sister or brother, as a friend—indeed,
in whatever role we have assumed. We carefully avoid
the disturbing thought that perhaps we could be doing a
better job than we are, or that there is so much in life that
we are losing by default or neglect. Sometimes, when we
get a bit closer to an uncomfortable revelation about ourselves, we satisfy our temporary discomfort by assuring

ourselves that we will get around to doing better as soon as we find the time. It is very important for us to understand this common weakness of self-deception because until we master it, we are mastered by it.

Since, in many instances, the truth about the kind of person you are is painful, you will stay away from it as far as possible. It is for this reason that many of us are so shocked when a day comes in which we are disillusioned with ourselves, with what we are doing, and with the people around us. Suddenly, we are engulfed by a terrible sense of inadequacy, and with bitterness we reflect upon the realization that we are alone. We don't seem to have the wisdom with which to appreciate life. We may have accumulated wealth, but it doesn't satisfy us. We may occupy a position of power, but our disposition is miserable. By the time we make this unhappy discovery, it is well nigh too late to begin to know how to find joy in living.

There is one direct way to know yourself and it is to do it on your own. Your best friends won't tell you. The people who make up your circle of acquaintances will not dare to describe you as you really are, even if they know. They probably talk about it to one another. Often people will say about someone, "He may be a successful businessman, but what a bore to have around. I wonder what he or she gets out of life?" Your so-called friends will dine with you and play with you, but they will not admit to you that they have no respect for your conduct.

I recall an incident during a visit to a small community wherein this fact was illustrated. The couple who met me gave me a swift profile of the leadership of the community and their conversation went something like this—"very rich, but very ignorant"; "An old family, but as tight as tight can be"; "So-and-so sounds all right, but try and get a contribution for charity from her"; "This man owes his position solely to the fact that he has money, but no one really respects him." To be sure, when these people assembled, they greeted one another most amiably and one could not tell from seeing this group together that privately they held such unfriendly thoughts toward one another.

The point I want to stress is that *you* must confront yourself in order to discover the truth about yourself, *you* must break down the barriers of self-deception and look fearlessly at what you are and compare it with what you know you really ought to be. If you are lucky enough to follow this advice at once, you will probably be in for a painful session with yourself, but you will also be able to begin to develop those capacities which God has given you and which will help you live significantly.

Now we are not denying that it is possible for people to go through a whole lifetime, to the day of their death, apparently getting by fairly well despite a wasteful existence. We see such people around us, wherever we go. The primary and virtually exclusive use to which these people put their leisure time is either to play cards, or to follow baseball or football, or to attend similar athletic events. The newspaper, to such people, is the sports page and the comics, which is the extent of their mental curiosity. None of these forms of relaxation are evil in themselves. Of course not. But they do become an evil when they are the sole interest, to the exclusion of all others, in the life of a person. We have not been so endowed with the divine gift of reason, with a mind to know and to understand and to see the wonders of the world, with a soul to grasp the glory of God, that we should paralyze our in-

tellect and spiritual capacities with the narcotic of squan-
dered, dissipated hours! What is there to distinguish us
from all other creatures on earth, if it be not this capacity
to think, to feel deeply, to stand on tiptoe before the
marvels and the mysteries of existence!

Not long ago, someone told me about a friend of hers,
who always finds the time during the year to read a book
in a field of learning about which he knows nothing. He
calls reading such a book, "stretching my mind." I don't
know this man, but I am as certain as I can be that he
doesn't ever feel alone. He can say with the poet, "My
mind to me a kingdom is; such present joys therein I
find." To exercise our mental resources becomes, then, an
essential responsibility of the human being who would
make of his life a pilgrimage of rewarding adventure.
To refuse to do this, intentionally or not, is to make ourselves vulnerable when we are overtaken by a crisis.

To me, one of the most rewarding concepts in the
teachings of Judaism is the description of man as God's
partner in working out our world's salvation. I think that
this, too, is what Jesus of Nazareth meant when he said,
"The Kingdom of God is within you." Jesus was born a
Jew, and raised in a Jewish home and trained in the lore of
Judaism. It is apparent that what Jesus meant was that it
is up to you and to me to shoulder our part of the responsibilities and the common task of making this world a better
place in which to live for all God's children. We may call
this cardinal teaching of Judaism the doctrine of supreme
partnership. God and man, together, working as partners
toward the thrilling goal of making this earth a province
of the Kingdom of Heaven. What an exalted position man
enjoys under this concept. He is not a helpless cog in the
wheel. He is not a dynamic bit of dust to be blown around

by the winds of fate. He is not a sinful, lowly, pitiful creature who can do nothing for himself but wait for some miracle to save him from being utterly forgotten and lost. On the contrary, to use the words of Holy Writ, man is made in God's own image. Man is dignified by his status as a free agent. If he wants to, he can work with God. But he can also shun this divine partnership and invite down upon himself catastrophe and ruin. With the knowledge that the Kingdom of God is within him, man must so live that the music and the ideals and the grandeur of God's Kingdom can come out, can be released, can be transposed into life and thus transform it. It is in this awareness of our supreme partnership, and by carrying our share of the burden of this partnership, that the ultimate conquest of loneliness can be achieved and the joyous awareness of participation in life can be won.

The writer of the Twenty-third Psalm must have been a man who knew suffering and pain and the loss of loved ones. He could have become an embittered cynic. He could have been so disillusioned by the knowledge that he was surrounded by enemies that he might have abandoned all faith and hope. He might have exclaimed, "This life is a mess, it is a tragedy, a disappointment. You love, and your beloved is taken away from you. You think you are fulfilling a dream and suddenly your dream is shattered. This life is not worth living, it is a lonely vigil that we keep until we die, and only death puts an end to our torments."

But he didn't say this. Instead, since he involved himself profoundly in the supreme partnership, he was able to say, "The Lord is my shepherd, I shall not want." And again he said, "Yea, though I walk through the valley of the shadow of death, I will fear no evil, for Thou art with me; Thy rod and Thy staff, they comfort me. Thou preparest a table before me in the presence of mine enemies." And then the most remarkable statement of all, as he cries "My cup runneth over." His cup of life holds more than a tiny drop; it is no empty, dry cup; it is not one-fourth filled, or one-half filled with meaning and joy, but it is a cup which runneth over, the brim overflowing with the thrill and the happiness of living. Such a man could, with justice, anticipate a significant life for himself. Holding fast to his faith in God, to his belief in God, to his understanding that he must work with God, he could face the future and say, "surely goodness and mercy shall follow me all the days of my life."

William Henry Channing, Chaplain of the House of Representatives in the middle of the last century, outlined a formula which is one of the finest for achieving the happiness of the supreme partnership, when he said the following:

"To live content with small means; to seek elegance rather than luxury, and refinement rather than fashion; to be worthy—to study hard, think quietly, talk gently, act frankly; to listen to the stars and birds, to babes and sages, with open heart; to bear all cheerfully, do all bravely, await occasions, hurry never; in a word to let the spiritual, unbidden and unconscious, grow up through the common."

No one else can do this for you. You must do it on your own, and once you do, you will have achieved a personal security which can triumph over loneliness; which can fill the days of your years with spiritual significance and the enjoyment of living.

One cannot, however, discuss supreme partnership without delving into that most important partnership between people which is marriage. Frequently this partnership proves to be a great disappointment. People will marry and have children and assume the responsibilities of family life, and yet be unsuccessful in knowing how to enjoy their marriage. Surely their longings are for a happy marriage, for successful parenthood, for significant family life. But much too often it doesn't work. What is the reason for so many marital and parental and family disasters? What are the essentials for a happy marriage, for being a successful mother or father; for creating those conditions in which family life can be enjoyed to the full?

CHAPTER VI

What Makes for a Happy Marriage?

I SHOULD LIKE to present here what seem to me to be the primary requirements for a happy marriage. I have come to these conclusions out of my own personal experience and study throughout my ministry.

Obviously, there must be attraction. We have to be drawn to each other. But far more important is mutual respect. We need to have respect for the other person's intellect, capacities and judgment. If a woman doesn't respect a man's intelligence and wisdom and his capacity to earn a living, then I am afraid that she will soon find him, regardless of his good looks, a very unattractive man. Equally, if a man comes to believe that a woman is inept, that she is a very poor manager of the home, that she has outlandish taste, that she is a miserable cook, that she lacks good judgment; then, regardless of her beauty, she becomes to him an unattractive female. Mutual respect, to me, is the first foundation stone upon which one can build the structure of successful marriage.

Unfortunately, it is difficult to convince young people nowadays that mutual respect is a most important qualification for happy marriage. To an alarming extent, young people believe that if they are physically attracted to someone, this will be quite enough on which to build a secure marriage. When we consider the glorifying of beauty in which the cinema indulges, which literature so frequently stresses, which most advertisements of fashion and style emphasize, it is not surprising that a pretty or handsome face is esteemed so highly.

Now let no one imagine for a moment that I am decrying the importance of attractive personal appearance. Indeed, it is a basic factor in human relationships. The very first question we ask about anyone is, "What does he or she look like?" But outer appearance should only be the introduction to one's knowledge of another person. Just being impressed with somebody's good looks is hardly a sound basis for marriage. Indeed, a charming personality is far more attractive than mere physical beauty. We all know people who are not good looking, but who are very popular and regarded to be most attractive primarily because of an ingratiating personality. Undoubtedly, we must look deeper, for appearance can be deceiving. We must know something about the intellectual strength, the mental vitality of the other person. If a marriage is to be happy, then the two people concerned should find one another intellectually stimulating. Without this quality, there is very little for the marriage to grow on and, sooner or later, that marriage becomes a humdrum affair. This doesn't mean that people have to be highly educated in order to develop a happy marriage. I am not inferring that the more degrees you have from college, the more chance there is that you will enjoy a better marriage. I am talking about common sense, native intelligence, down-to-earth realism and that marvelous capacity to know what is significant and what is unimportant. If a person says, "My wife is extravagant," then it is possible to rectify this mistake. Or someone declares, "My husband spends too much time on outside activities"—this can be altered for the better. Or should someone say, "We don't get along with one another's relatives" or "we suffer from physical incompatibility"—all these very serious problems can, under the right direction, be helped and corrected. But, if we hear, "My husband or wife is stupid" or "I have no respect for his or her judgment," then the situation is extremely difficult. Mutual respect, the respect for the other person's mind, the respect for the other person's all-around ability to do a good job of whatever it may be that one is doing—this is the first essential requirement for the happy marriage.

However, mutual respect is only the first essential. There must also be an awareness of unselfish, self-sacrificing love. Both the husband and wife must feel that to each other they come first in all considerations. If you are married and you are led to believe that you are not the end in itself, but a means to an end, that the other person married you for a selfish motive, then your marriage can never be happy. There is a popular belief that love comes first, above all other considerations, in the life of a woman, whereas a career is the first love of the man. But, in a happy marriage, love must come first for both wife and husband.

Of course, there are many, many marriages which survive and are what you might call "good marriages," in which careers are regarded to be of greater importance than one's wife, and, likewise, there are many marriages in which a woman regards her social career to be more important than her husband. But who would call this the true happy marriage? Would you? In a happy marriage, you know that you come first, regardless of what is involved. It is a source of unlimited joy to a husband or a wife, knowing that his or her happiness is the supreme objective of his or her mate. This is beautifully expressed in the following exquisite phrase from that wonderful love poem of the Bible called "Song of Songs," "I am my beloved's and my beloved is mine. . . ."

There is no obstacle in the path of a marriage which cannot be overcome when two people have this kind of unselfish relationship and when they possess this unique strength of self-sacrificing love. Those who get married for lesser reasons, because they think they ought to be married, or to provide themselves with a meal-ticket, or to gain some social standing or, no matter what the particular motive may be, those who marry with ulterior purposes in mind, will find marriage a disappointment and will never know the real glory of a profoundly satisfying romance.

Consider, too, that a basic essential for a happy marriage is compatibility. Nowadays when we mention compatibility we usually mean physical or sexual compatibility. Important as this is, it is only one vital part of a larger mosaic of blending interest consisting, for example, of the enjoyment of the same kind of people, the same kind of ideas and books. If two young people want to be certain to find their marriage in the divorce court, let them have very few interests in common, let them be poles apart, opposites in their sense of humor, in their spiritual values, in their social interests. The happiest marriages are those marriages in which the parties concerned have most in common. Opposites may attract but they are poor marital risks. In a happy marriage there is such a strong degree of sympathy and empathy between husband and wife that often they anticipate one another's wants without the necessity of speaking about them. There is very little need for explanations. They communicate with one another even in their silences.

This does not mean that the individuality of the husband and wife in a happy marriage must be obscured. When we say that compatibility means a blending of interests and the enjoyment of the same kind of people and books and things, we still leave much room for what the poet Kahlil Gibran describes as "spaces in your togetherness." Surely we do not expect people to surrender their own claim to original personality when they get married. We do not wish the husband or the wife to become shadows of their former selves. The truth is that if a marriage is a happy one, it will bring out the very finest and the best, the highest and the noblest in the individuals concerned.

Moreover, a happy marriage releases the husband and wife from bondage to that tense phase of social competition in which men and women strive, at all cost, to win the special favor of each other. The unmarried person and the unhappily married person are looking for someone who will live up to their ideal. They are out to make a conquest or to attract to themselves the interest of a member of the opposite sex. Hence they cannot be at ease and at liberty to enjoy other people for themselves alone. For this choice prize belongs to those who are happily married. Having found and married the one you love deeply and truly, you are free to make the maximum contribution toward living and working in pure friendship with the opposite sex. Both husband and wife who are physically and spiritually and mentally compatible are united in a great comradeship, to be sure, but it is the kind of comradeship which makes of them better citizens, better human beings, infinitely better people who add to the happiness of those around them.

There is another foundation of extreme importance for the happy marriage. It is the controlled temper. Being human, all of us have tempers. However, some of us have more than others. But all of us should learn to control our tempers. Many a marriage has been ruined through the misery caused by violent outbursts of rage. In a temper we say and do things we bitterly regret in calm moods. The uncontrolled temper deprives us of our capacity to meet the inevitable problems of marriage with sagacity and confidence. When these vexing problems overtake us in marriage it requires all of our mature and tranquil judgment to meet and solve them satisfactorily. Furthermore, a bad temper, leading as it does to abuses and insults, name-calling and ugly arguments, quarrels, discourtesies and vile selfishness, breeds so much evil that it often makes of marriage a shambles, drains it of all its lofty meaning and beauty.

Lest you think that I am not being realistic and that I am forgetting that we are human and not angels, let me recount the following amusing story: "At the golden wedding anniversary of a happy couple, the husband was called upon to speak and this is what he said, 'Ladies and gentlemen. Many of you have complimented me tonight on my healthy and ruddy complexion, my youthful appearance. Let me tell you the secret of it. When we first married, my wife and I agreed that, whenever either of us felt a fit of temper coming on, that we would go out and take a walk until the temper cooled off. Ladies and gentlemen, that is why I have this healthy sunburned look; I have spent much of the time of my fifty years of marriage walking in the sunshine.' " This story contains a very good lesson for all of us. Situations are bound to arise in marriage which irritate and disturb us. When this happens, I plead with you to control that temper, do anything to suppress it, take a walk, count to ten, do anything except permit your temper to come to the surface. A controlled disposition is one of the blessed attributes of the happy marriage.

Undoubtedly a primary cause for marital discord is fatigue. Yes, fatigue! Most of us don't bother to analyze it but the fact remains that fatigue plays a large part in all that we do. The medical world has not, as yet, explained the physiological reasons for fatigue beyond the presentation of several interesting theories. Perhaps fatigue is due to lactic acid formed in the tissues; or it is brought on by a toxin produced by the brain tissue which acts as a soporific; or does the pituitary put us to sleep? These chemical theories and many others are advanced by scientists. No one has yet found the answer which is final. Nevertheless, it is true that after a certain amount of activity and so many hours of just being awake, we become tired, sleepy, listless. As fatigue begins to overpower us, we become less efficient, slower, duller in our senses and sensibilities. We struggle to overcome fatigue, yet in the struggle we grow wearier and more irritable. Certainly when we are fatigued we are not ourselves. We don't notice much, nor do we care. Sometimes we are so overtired that we can't sleep. We are nervous, mean, highstrung.

In the marriage relationship, fatigue, like any other physical change, affects our thinking and action. A physiological condition modifies our psychological state, and vice versa. Modern medicine is fascinated by this process, and calls it by the word "psychosomatic." The thoughts of the mind affect the body. The condition of the body affects the mind. Thus when a husband or wife at any time is fatigued, he or she is not quite normal. The fatigued person, who otherwise is bright and charming, is now indifferent, laconic, unattentive, provokingly dull. Certainly the physically exhausted person is in no mood for giving or receiving ardent and loving attention.

Consider this example. John comes home exhausted. Mary is wearing a new dress and her hair-style is changed. She has tried to make herself most attractive and anticipates the compliments and warm approval of her beloved husband. But John has walked in with hardly a mumble of a word of greeting. Usually he notices everything. Tonight—nothing. "What is wrong?" Mary asks herself most anxiously. "Maybe this dress is unbecoming and my hair-do is silly. What have I done? Has he met someone else? Why this change? Why this coldness, this indifference?" Alas for this needless torture. Her husband is only fatigued. He is played-out, and that is why he doesn't notice her new dress nor say the endearing word.

Similarly, when a husband or wife feels ill, there is bound to be a psychological change. How foolish not to tell each other what is wrong. Why create misunderstanding because you would spare one another any apprehension? This is misguided comradeship. Speak up! Tell your beloved, "I am weary, completely exhausted," or, "I have a headache or a toothache," or whatever it is. Then your spouse will be spared unhappy thoughts and distressing conclusions. Then there will be sympathy and unity and helpfulness. When fatigue overtakes you, admit it and say so. Go to sleep, which is the only cure for your fatigue. Don't make yourself go out or stay up. Good heavens, here is one thing over which we can exercise direct control! It is madness to permit fatigue to cause so much trouble in marriage when we can eliminate its harmful repercussions by remembering that it is a factor with which to reckon. But, unfortunately, being raised on a heavy diet of romantic expectations, we are reluctant to admit that we are fatigued lest it be a sign of age or weakness. Thus, we invite needless misery into our married life. Try this simple technique of telling your dear one when you are fatigued, that you feel tired. Then retire early. You will both be happier and remove from your marriage unnecessary unpleasantness and discord.

Husbands need to be reminded here how to avoid another serious emotional complication in marriage. The fact is that each month, during her menstrual cycle, a woman is emotionally on edge; some women are more so than others. All women are affected emotionally to a greater or less degree by the menses period. A husband during those days should forebear bringing up differences and desist from introducing incendiary discussions. It is nothing short of criminal for a man to provoke his wife in any manner during her menstrual term. She should be favored and spared unnecessary excitement for that period. A man who will not accept this discipline of caution takes unfair advantage of his wife. He also hurts himself, for in an emotional outburst of his wife's fury, at that time of the month, he jeopardizes their chance for a happy marriage.

There is another discipline which both husband and wife should accept completely if their marriage is to be successful. This is to resist the temptation to talk down or to berate the wife's or husband's family. Beware of this temptation. It can come at you, for example, in the following manner. Often you talk to each other in that unique intimacy of marriage during which your minds and hearts think and beat in unison. At least you think so or are led to believe this is true. At this point you hear your wife complain about her mother. How she will despise the selfish, thoughtless, mean woman! How she will carry on against her mother's refusal to help when asked! And so on and on. You listen and you want to agree. In fact, you don't need to be persuaded by logic or evidence. For a long time you have been aware of your mother-in-law's genius for making trouble. At precisely this point in your thinking I warn you to keep your mouth shut! But tightly and firmly closed! Don't say a word! By all that is holy, keep silent, for if you speak out and agree by even so much as a trifle, or you are reckless enough to add your own list of grievances, then you have really asked for it! You will notice a strange, chilled look come over the face of your darling wife. And it won't be friendly. She will then suddenly turn on you like a wounded tigress. She will shout: "How dare you say that about my wonderful mother! How dare you, of all people in the world, call her selfish! If you want to see how terribly selfish a woman can be then look at your own mother!" Thus will the battle rage and storm, a battle which would never be fought if one only remembered the simple caution that one should never say a word when the other person is complaining against his or her folks. Never forget that "blood is thicker than water." You feel that you have the right to say what you like about your own family. For you are speaking about *your* mother, or *your* father, or *your* sister and brother. You belong to them. You are part of them. You love them and because you do not question your love for them you feel free to criticize them as you will. But this is *your* right and not the right of this stranger who happens to be your husband or wife. He or she is not bound by ties of blood. He or she is an outsider.

I plead with you, then, to let your beloved rave on and on against his or her family. Say nothing and do nothing.

The very next minute the phone may ring and it will be your maligned mother-in-law. How sweetly and affectionately will "mama" be greeted by your spouse who but a moment ago was declaiming that mama is hateful. After all is said and done, "mama" is still "mama."

I wonder how long it is going to take for us to realize that people don't just get married and then happiness results automatically. A happy marriage is created, directed, nurtured, developed. It takes a lot of effort to make marriage a success. It requires the ability to keep from taking one another for granted. It demands that we let nothing stand in the way of making our marriage a success. We need consideration for each other, we need a sense of humor. Above all, the happy marriage must be the goal we seek with all of our hearts and souls. That it is worthwhile, no one can deny, for a happy marriage means a happy home, happy children. A happy marriage represents the fulfillment of our dreams, the joy of great companionship, of perfect partnership. Let all those who are about to be married, and all those who are married, recognize the solemn responsibilities of marriage. It is by no means a relationship to be entered into lightly, nor can it be successful without serious effort.

In Hebrew, the word for marriage is "kedushin," which literally translated doesn't mean marriage at all, but "sanctification." Perhaps that is the clue to the happy marriage; this idea that marriage is sanctification—the sanctification of the commonplace, the sanctification of our animal desires, the sanctification of life itself. Of all the goals in life worth winning, greater than fame and fortune, greater than any mundane power or glory we know, is the happy marriage founded upon mutual respect, the controlled disposition, compatibility and unselfish love. And what is more, there is no better way to achieve the world of peace we all desire. For when men and women are happily married, they are inspired mentally and spiritually to believe in and to strive for the realization of the blessings of justice and brotherly love among all mankind.

We have not discussed thus far the crowning glory of marriage, which is parenthood. How does one become the kind of mother or father who is a blessing to one's children? As we confront next the challenge of motherhood and fatherhood, we shall find, I trust, some helpful counsel and criticism.

CHAPTER VII

The Challenge of Motherhood

EACH YEAR, Americans celebrate Mother's Day. We know that throughout the United States millions of dollars are spent to purchase gifts and flowers and candy by children of all ages in honor of their mothers. Many people object to the commercial features of Mother's Day. However justified, such criticism overlooks the fact that these mercantile aspects help considerably to make Mother's Day a powerful institution in American life.

There is something thrilling about a whole nation alerted to the thought of motherhood and its great sanctity. It is always a good thing to take the time to show one's appreciation and love, one's gratitude for favors. How much more is it good for us to pause and pay homage to our mothers. Of course there is the danger of being too gushy and sweet on Mother's Day. It is not easy to resist the temptation to exaggerate beyond any semblance of reality how affectionate we feel toward her who brought us into this world and raised us. On the other hand, we can be so zealous for restraint that we do not manifest enough of our sentiments toward motherhood. We shall avoid the extremes, as we concern ourselves with the challenge of motherhood today.

I want to make it clear that I am fully cognizant of the enormity of the thousand and one tasks which the modern mother is called upon to do. When I think of what a mother is expected to be in order to do her job success-fully, I simply marvel at her resourcefulness and her ca-pacity. Compared with what we fathers do, and are expected to do, the work of motherhood is infinitely more complex and demanding. A father leaves his home in the morning and he goes to his work which is usually con-fined to some specialty. Whether a man be in a business or a profession, he does that job and nothing else; he is an expert in his particular activity and he is able to concen-trate on his special task without any interference.

The mother, however, has an endless variety of respon-sibilities to meet. In the great chorale of life, the father sings a solo, whereas the mother must be able to sing many parts of the music. To be a successful mother to-day, a woman is supposed to be a loving wife to her hus-band, and a devoted mother to her children. She must be a child psychologist, an economist, a decorator, civic worker, church worker, and educator. She must know how to cook, wash, iron, clean house, sew, knit, repair, nurse, and comfort. She must be a counselor, adviser, peace maker, and informed citizen, a devotee of the arts, a charming conversationalist, a well-dressed and attrac-tive woman—all of this and more at one and the same time. In a single day, a mother must meet every kind of emergency, ranging from domestic crises to problems of Church and State. That she is able to do all of these—or some of these as well as she does—and that she sometimes fails to do some of these things successfully, and that she still keeps her sense of humor and sanity, is all quite im-pressive.

Not long ago there was a very delightful play pre-sented in New York called "Life with Mother." Within a period of two hours, this drama deals with the amazing complexity and variety of a mother's responsibilities as she helps her husband and four boys to meet their problems, while at the same time she solves her own. The mother in this play, like some mothers in real life, affects the mannerisms of a scatterbrained, naive person who apparently doesn't know what things are all about. Nevertheless, in her own way, she manages to accomplish exactly what she wants—nothing more and nothing less. There is a method to Mother's madness, which all good children in good time come to recognize and to honor. You come away from that play realizing that you should never underestimate a mother, especially if that mother has a definite objective in view. It must have been a mother who thought up the old proverb, "There are more ways than one to skin a cat." Once a mother makes up her mind about something she wants, or doesn't want, for her husband, herself, her children, or her home, nothing this side of God's Heaven can stop her. A mother is a power, and never fool yourself that she isn't. Next to God, she is the greatest power on earth.

Now, it is precisely because a mother can exercise such a potent influence in the home that we ask her to exercise her power in behalf of saving our civilization. I quote here some words of Dr. Ashley Montagu, Professor of Anthropology at Rutgers University, from his article, "The Mothers of Mankind":

"Unless men learn from women how to be more loving and co-operative, they will go on making the kind of mess of the world which they have so effectively achieved thus far.

"And this is, of course, where women can realize their power for good in the world, and make their greatest gains. *It is the function of women to teach men how to be human.* Women must not permit themselves to be deviated from this function by those who tell them that their place is in the home in subservient relation to man. It is, indeed, in the home that the foundations of the kind of world in which we live are laid, and in this sense it will always remain true that the hand that rocks the cradle is the hand that rules the world. And it is in this sense that women must assume the job of making men, who will know how to make a world fit for human beings to live in. The greatest single step forward in this direction will be made when women consciously assume this task—the task of teaching their children to be like themselves, loving and co-operative."

We can agree wholeheartedly with Dr. Montagu, and agree just as completely with what he says later on in this article, when in summing up the essence of scientific discoveries in the field of mother-child relationship, he stated, "The one thing the child must have in order to live is oxygen, and next in importance to oxygen is mother love."

Suppose you asked several people: "What is the essence of the greatness of mother love?" The answers would vary to a large extent, with many different kinds of emphasis placed upon various qualities. Some would say that real mother love means to raise law-abiding children. Others might hold that mothers should teach their children to be religious, and still others would opine that the major function of the mother is to organize the kind of home which is happy, pleasant, a refuge from the world outside. No doubt, there is much to be said for all these ideas, but my own opinion stresses what seems to me to be the foundation of all manifestations of healthy mother love. My belief is that the essence of the greatness of mother love is her willingness to give sacrificially to the welfare of her children. How clearly is this truth revealed in a recent selection of the American Mother of the Year. She is a slight, gray-haired Chinese mother of eight talented children. She lives in Portland, Maine, and her name is Mrs. Toy Lem Goon, a widow in her late fifties. She operates a laundry, and works arduously. Of her children, one is a physician, another a scientist, others are teachers and businessmen. With Lincoln, each of these fine children can say, "All that I am or hope to be, I owe to my angel mother."

Here then, we have the perfect example of the ideal mother, the woman who places her children's welfare first. This, to me, is the highest virtue of motherhood. Conversely, the essence of the greatest evil in a mother is her refusal to place her children first in every situation. The one is loving attention, the other is selfish neglect. If you will look, with me, at the modern mother in this light, we may come to some conclusion that may prove to be helpful.

Those of you who have kept up with the literature of psychologists and psychiatrists must be impressed with their unanimous conclusion that the first six years in a person's life are the most important. The experiences of childhood, we are told by every authority, influence our character and personality development. Most failures in life are due, then, not so much to deficiencies in intelligence and capacities as they are to our personality problems whose source is found in the first six years of life.

It is to be profoundly deplored that in our modern world, very often, the career of being a mother seems to occupy a second place to the career in the business or the professional world. Perhaps the greatest price we have had to pay for the emancipation of the modern woman from drudgery is a self-centered, egocentric society which is incapable of making the mature decisions of co-opera- tion and unity. Throughout my ministry I have observed that a chief reason for the tension in family life—between husband and wife, for example—is the stress that is put on what we think is due to us, not on what we ought to be doing for somebody else. Inevitably, the maladjustment in the marriage reveals itself as being essentially a question of selfishness or unselfishness. I recall an unhappy woman saying, "When I look around and see what other wives are getting, I know that I am being taken advantage of, that my husband is indifferent to my needs." And I have heard a husband say, "My wife doesn't offer me the kind of home that other men get. She is much more interested in our social life than in our private life."

There are many reasons for divorce and unhappiness in marriage, but it all leads down to one dismal conclusion, which is that men and women who are emotionally im- mature, who fail to show self-sacrificing love for one another, are ineligible to be the kind of mates, and later the kind of parents, we need in order to heal the wounds of our society. The mother is unworthy of the honor of being a mother who rebels against her duties, her tasks, her responsibilities in the home, which, so to speak, tie her down to it. Her attitude of revolt against being tied down to the home has reduced her home to being a mere dormi- tory. Too many of our homes are where we sleep and eat, but not where human beings meet, and through their ex- periences in the home, become prepared for mature, use- ful and happy living outside the home.

I do not wish to underestimate the importance of the father. Indeed, it is to be lamented that the modern father is hardly ever at home enough to get to know his children. No doubt, the pressures of making a living, of economic necessities, force the fathers of our time into the role of a "visiting uncle," or of a boarder, or just the man who is seen briefly in the evening. Even then, what with radio and television, there is very little chance for a father to talk with his children. That is why so much stress has to be placed on the role of a mother in the home. She is the one who is in the first line of relationship to the child. She gives birth to the child, nurtures it, develops it, and in the normal order of events, is much more in contact with the child. Should mothers object that we are expecting too much of them, we can reply that our life is such that they are the ones to whom we must turn for responsible action in this crucial problem of creating the kind of homes in which finer human beings can be developed. To be sure, a good job is being done with regard to the superficial aspects of the child's needs. The modern mother sees to it that her child goes to school and has lots of opportunity for play. She takes care, as best she can, of the physical needs of her child. The modern child certainly gets lots of entertainment. He learns how to dance and to play and to swim. He is taught to train his muscles to develop a healthy body. But the most important part of the modern child is neglected when he doesn't have the mother who takes the time to help him develop his character and personality so that he is trained in the art of living happily with other people.

There is no greater evidence of this truth than in the fact that children who come from the most privileged homes in terms of money, of wealth, are very often conspicuous failures in marriage, in friendship, in every kind of human relationship. The Bible tells us, in a very telling phrase, what is at the root of the failure in people's lives who have everything material and nothing more. The Bible says, "Jesurun waxed fat and he kicked." This is to say that when we grow rich, when we have wealth, when we are abundantly cared for materially, we tend to revolt against, that is, we kick against and we neglect spiritual values. There seems to be a distinct co-relation between material prosperity alone and spiritual impoverishment. When will our mothers understand that it is far more important to give themselves to their children, especially in the early years, than to give their children another toy, or an increase in their allowance, another dress, another party. Not that we should overlook the superficial needs of our children. But, when this materialistic concern becomes the substitute for our first responsibility, which is spiritual and qualitative, then there is the devil to pay.

I would be grossly misunderstood if I were to leave the impression with you that the modern mother goes out of her way to harm her children, to deprive them of what they need spiritually. This is entirely remote from any thought that I have on the subject. What I do mean to convey is that the modern mother has permitted herself to be misled by false standards of successful living. Surely, she loves her child as any mother in any generation has. Be it further noted, that in few eras have mothers had to suffer so much as in our own. In our lifetime—two world wars, and the Korean war, have brought untimely death to our youth, and only the mother's heart knows what this sorrow means. In our generation, many mothers not only have suffered the loss of their sons killed in war, but also they must rear their children in a world which is trembling in the balance of life or death. There is a neurotic tinge and the tightness of strain in almost everything we do. Thus it is not surprising that the sense of insecurity, of uncertainty, the fear of another World War should all communicate their fitful fevers to our children in our homes.

There is nothing more difficult to achieve in the world today than to be a successful mother, because the odds are so much against the mother. She would teach her children peace; instead, the radio, the newspapers, the movies, the events of our lives teach them war and violence. The true mother would teach her children to be sincere and thoughtful; but society teaches her children, too frequently, that hypocrisy and insincerity seem to make their way in the world with very little hindrance. Yet, the very gravity of the general picture, as difficult as it makes the task of motherhood, nevertheless poses the greatest challenge ever faced by mothers in the history of mankind. As never before, we need mothers who will resist the evils of our age, who will accept as the greatest goal in life the rearing of children who will add to the goodness and the beauty and the peace of our times.

I remember standing by the bedside of a veteran who was dying from wounds sustained in the recent war. He was unconscious—silent—but just before he died, he said one word, and that word sent a shiver up the spines of the doctors and the nurses—all of us standing around that bed. That poor boy's last word was "Mother." Many men and women have gone to their Maker with that word on their lips, for of all the words of our language, it is the most sacred, next to the name of God.

I implore every mother reading this chapter to know that she stands as the representative of God in our homes. In a thrilling and terrible sense, she has the power of life and death over her children, because she can mold her children into the kind of people who know how to live the Godly life, or live the destructive life. May there come a realization to every mother that a glorious new world of happiness is waiting to be born, whose birth depends upon them. The challenge of motherhood today is to bring forth the kind of men and women who are worthy to enter that Golden Age of universal justice and enduring peace.

CHAPTER VIII

The Modern Father

FROM THE SUBJECT of motherhood, let us turn our attention to the man who is the modern father. Let me ask the following question concerning father: to what extent is the modern father doing the job he should as the head of his household? By this I mean, how close is he to his children, how much time does he give to them, what kind of example is he?

I, for one, feel that the modern father is perhaps in the most unenviable position of any father in history. He loves his children. He enjoys family union. He likes to be a friend to his children, a guide and a comrade. The modern father would be most pleased to spend a great deal of time with his children and really develop that kind of relationship which makes for the finest and happiest family life. But, alas, as much as the modern father wants to do all these things, he is not in a position to do so because his work keeps him away from his home. He is absent from early morning until the dinner hour. His children have some of their most important experiences without even a sign of father around the house. Moreover, his work is usually such as to bring him home mentally fatigued, and wanting peace and relaxation, rather than to assume the challenge of being an interesting companion to his offspring.

When father comes home from work, he is in no mood to deal with the whims of his children. He is irritable because he is tired and hungry and often worried. He is scarcely ready to help junior with his lessons. He cannot but find himself out of place in the exciting life of his children, who associate themselves, because she is always there and at hand, more intimately with their mother. When the dinner is over and father feels, perhaps, somewhat relaxed and rested, he cannot attract his children because they are at the radio or television set, and quite cold to a discussion of school problems or anything else.

I am sure that there are a number of exceptions to what I have just stated. There are some fathers, because of the nature of the work they do, or because they are the kind of men that they are, who do have ample time for their children. This I believe to be the exception and not the rule. In the majority of cases, children seldom have much contact with their father so that the larger part of the responsibility of raising the children must be met by the mother. If I have been fair in my portrayal of this particular aspect of family life, and I hope I have, then I believe it would be in order to ask ourselves what the modern father can do to derive from his family life, as well as to contribute to it, at least some of the good, the joy, and the blessing that it should contain.

I observed above that I feel sorry for the modern father. He has to work all day under pressure. He works so hard that he usually dies many years before his wife, and thus there is this tragic aspect to his existence. According to actuarial statistics, men die, on the average, from five to seven years before their wives. A man has to meet the rigors of tough competition, has to work hard to get to the top, has to work hard in any case, if only to support his family. He does not get enough of the abiding happiness of life. Working these days, at most jobs, is not much fun because of its hectic tempo. The average man has little opportunity to interest himself in the things of the spirit because he is so busy providing enough fuel to keep the home fires burning. While the life of the mother is also full of hardships, as I described it in the previous chapter, she derives many satisfactions from her daily experiences. This appraisal, I know, goes contrary to the popular idea that this is a man's world. From what I have seen, this only *appears* to be a man's world. Actually, men work their lives away trying to give a portion of this world to their mothers, wives and children. They come home mentally, if not physically, exhausted. They need rest. Because I understand this, I have told my Congregation, several times, that I do not object to men falling asleep at the service. I think the relaxation does them a great deal of good, and if coming to God's Sanctuary can provide them with that kind of peace which they can't seem to get anywhere else, why then that's perfectly all right with me.

If I have drawn a picture of the modern father which makes of him a rather weary and troubled kind of human being, a person who goes to work and comes home unready for family or cultural experiences, I may be guilty of exaggerating the picture a trifle, but I don't think it is too far from the mark. Most fathers that I meet haven't the time to develop that understanding of their child's aptitude and problems which is so essential for the proper guidance of young people.

I once asked a grandfather whether the popular saying is true, that grandparents love their grandchildren as much as, if not more than, their own children. He replied that grandfathers feel unusually close to their grandchildren because, as grandfathers, they have more time to give to these children than they had for their own during the very busy years when they were actively engaged in the business of making a living. There you have it again—the need for time in order to enjoy the blessings of life.

Somehow, one cannot escape the feeling that a large part of the chaos of our modern world is due to the inability of the modern father to play the part he should in his home. If the psychologists are right when they maintain that belief in God comes easy to the person who has been close to and loves his father, then perhaps the widespread lack of interest in religion in our time may be partially explained by the fact that the modern child experiences very little with his father. In the olden days, we had an age of faith—the age of belief. But those were the days when father came home at noontime, when life was slower, when outside distractions were at a minimum, when father and mother and the children were close to the soil, and worked as a unit together. In those days, barring droughts or floods, a family could enjoy that security which comes to those who rely upon the soil to produce the food they need to eat in order to live. There was a real sense of economic freedom then. The father didn't have to worry about money as the only means whereby he could provide food and shelter for his children. In those days, they grew the things they needed. They also made the clothes they wore, so that there was a tremendous sense of independence which added to the dignity and the strength and the freedom of the home. Today, when the father who works in a factory, or in a store, or in some job, gets laid off, or if he loses his money, it may mean starvation for his family. His wages, today, must do all that in former times the farm and the soil did for the family. Consequently, the modern father worries so much more, is dependent so much more on others for his economic livelihood. No wonder he is bound to his job and expends his energies on his work, because it makes all the difference between going with and going without, for himself, his wife and children.

I want to stress this, because I don't think enough of us appreciate what has happened to the modern family in our mechanized, electric-atomic power age because of economic dependence. Modern man is not free, the way his grandfather was free who lived on a farm and who could always grow enough for himself and dependents to keep from going hungry. The modern man, and the modern father, must rely upon many outside sources for the keeping of body and soul together for himself and for his dear ones. Thus, there is a tension in modern life—a fear, a worry, which saps the vitality of the modern father. We should not be surprised that security rather than freedom is the greatest objective sought by modern man. Let us recognize these things, in order to be more sympathetic to the problems we all share in common. Also, let us *understand* this, so that perhaps we shall be able to take a constructive attitude toward our problem and solve it for our mutual good.

Since the modern father has so little time to be with his children, then let him use wisely whatever time he does have, and share it with his sons and daughters. It is a nice thing to see a father taking his son with him on a fishing trip, or on some special vacation jaunt. We ought to do this as often as we can, and realize how precious and wonderful this opportunity is. Unfortunately, these opportunities come very seldom. But there is an opportunity which comes once a week, which I believe every father ought

to take advantage of without fail. I refer to coming to the
House of God on the Sabbath with one's children. I know
that the Sabbath day is a day on which father would much
rather take it easy, or work in the yard, or play golf, or
do almost anything to get away from the vexing thought
of business, and of making a living. Do those things in the
afternoon, fathers, but give the morning of the Sabbath
day, or some period of the Sabbath, to visiting the House
of God with your children. It will provide you with the
opportunity of sharing something great with your loved
ones. You will be an example to your children of religious
devotion. You will bring your children closer to ethical
and moral teachings. There is nothing healthier for the
mind and body of each member of the family than to learn
to believe in God, to trust in Him, and to walk in His
ways.

The students of family life, the child psychologists who
are specialists in the field of parent-child relationship, may
differ on many points, but on one fact they are all united.
They agree that the major cause for maladjustment in the
lives of children is due to what they call "Child Rejection."
I am sure that this must be quite shocking to most fathers
and mothers who cannot understand how any parent could
reject a child. And yet the case histories of juvenile delin-
quents prove that more children than we like to admit suffer from being rejected by their parents, by being made
to feel unwanted, being denied that parental love without
which it is almost impossible for a child to grow up sound
in mind and body. Now, child rejection takes on many
aspects—very often parents unconsciously do those things
which warp the healthy spiritual growth of a child. Parents who are away from home a great deal in the evenings,
by accepting innumerable social engagements to the detri-

ment of their children—parents who don't go out of their way to get to know their offspring, to show their love, are rejecting their children.

Do not imagine for one moment that a child is satisfied with just a gift or a treat on some special occasion. No matter how much a boy or girl seems to be involved in his or her activities, they are keenly aware of the presence or the absence of their parents. Not long ago, I asked a little boy to carry a message home to his mother. Whereupon he replied, "I think it will be better if you call her this evening, because she is never home when I come back from school." That child is already feeling rejection! Just the other day, I asked a boy to speak to his father that night, on some plans for our religious school. He answered, "Please call Dad at his office, because I seldom see him in the evening, and when he is home it is hard to get to talk to him." That child, too, has begun to feel rejection!

Our country needs inner spiritual strength if it is to survive in this critical era. We cannot be certain of survival if we turn our backs on family life. The ancient country of Greece, in all of its glory, in all of its magnificence of art and culture, went down in defeat in large measure because divorce, sexual immorality and contempt for family life had broken the strength of that great nation. The same tragic pattern was carried out in Rome when with moral degeneracy and contempt for family life, the grandeur of Rome was destroyed from within because of a spiritual decay. Our beloved country need not fear for its future if we, the people, restore family life to that healthy condition which has always been the backbone of our democracy. If only more families would associate themselves intimately with their sanctuary, with the church of their choice and with the minister of the church, what a boon this would bring into family life. In a world where there is so little time to appreciate and to grasp hold of the eternal values, how eager we should be to make use of whatever opportunities remain to share with our children in that uplifting experience which comes only from being at home in the House of God.

I would like to see fathers and children go out of their way to find the opportunity to be together whenever possible. May I stress this especially with regard to fathers and sons, for it is essential in these days that they share as many experiences as they can. We live in a time of war, of the preparation for war. We live in a time when boys, by the age of eighteen, leave for military training. They will be away from home. Then it will be impossible for fathers and sons to be together. Once the boy leaves home, it is too late to seek him out and to be his friend, his guide and beloved comrade. I think that the modern father should be zealous to find and to seize every opportunity to be with his children—to be a wise father who knows his children—to be a loving father who loves his children.

He will find that his children are waiting for him. He will learn that his children are yearning for him and seek his love. This poignant truth is revealed in the following incident which occurred one night in the lives of a father and his little son. The boy was ill and asked for the privilege of sleeping with his father. The father replied, "Of course, my son. We shall sleep together and in the morning you will be all better." Some time passed as they lay there in the darkness. The father thought that surely the lad had fallen asleep, for the child was quiet and seemed to be breathing evenly. Suddenly the little boy spoke up and said, "Father, is your face turned toward me?" And his father answered, "Yes, my son, why do you ask?" "Oh,

I just wanted to be sure that your face is turned toward me. It makes me feel better to know that. Now I can sleep."

Every son needs a father whose face is turned toward him, a father who, despite all the obstacles of modern living, nevertheless turns his face toward his children in love and devotion, in faith and peace. Every day of the year, let all families thank God for the blessing which is theirs. Let all resolve to take advantage of every opportunity of getting closer together, of loving one another dearly, of rejoicing in the sanctity of family union. For in the peace and strength of family life our nation shall have peace and strength. And in the peace and strength of the nation, our world can come nearer to the attainment of universal peace.

CHAPTER IX

The Future Is Our Children

To BOTH FATHERS AND MOTHERS I put the following questions: What kind of a future do you want to see for America? What sort of life do you hope to have developed in the days to come? Are we not all in accord with that dream of an America which is spiritually strong, prosperous and happy—an America at peace with the world in a world at peace? Are not all of us who are parents yearning for a future in which our children may live lives that are courageous, ethical, creative and pacific?

Surely most of us want that kind of future for our children and for our beloved country. On this point, if on no other, our choice is quite unanimous. Well then, since this is so, let me ask you where is this future to be found? How are you going to make such a future real? How will you take the dream out of the skies of aspiration to make it come true on this earth? There is, it seems to me, one certain way to do this. It is to realize the simple truth that the future is our children—right now, in the very present. The future is not tomorrow, about which we are ignorant; it is not a date far ahead on the calendar. The future is with us; we see it in our children; we are molding it and forming it every day as we influence their lives. That is why we parents show a terrible lack of foresight when we fail to give our children all those opportunities for

mental and spiritual and character growth which are so
essential for the realization of our dream.

First of all, we want parents to give more of themselves
to their children. We delegate too many responsibilities to
others. We leave it entirely to somebody else to provide
them with knowledge, with entertainment, to stimulate
them, to give them goals and ambitions. All these other
agencies for religion and education and guidance and inspiration are most important and fundamental. The trouble, however, lies in the fact that too many parents feel
that their job is over when they have placed the child in
a position of exposure to these influences. Now, we would
not underestimate the importance of the teacher and the
school. Nevertheless, the school is but one of the great
social agencies which help to mold the future by influenc-
ing the child. We parents have our children with us much
more of the time than does the school. Nor should we underestimate the importance of the minister and the church.
Obviously, the institutions of organized religion can, and
often do, play a tremendous role in the moral development of our children. Yet, here too, the church and synagogue can only be the assistants to the parents, can, at best,
but emphasize those ideals which ought to be taught in the
home.

The qualified psychologists tell us, as we have previ-
ously noted, that the first six years are the most important
in the life of the individual. Thus it should be almost painfully clear that parents, and parents above all, must assume
the responsibility for the kind of people our children become. What a tragedy that we allow ourselves to become
so involved with social and financial obligations that we
don't find the time to be teachers to our children. We seem
to be saying, "Let the minister give our children religion.

Let the teachers educate them. Let them learn from other children how to get along."

But our children, in the beginning at least, look to us as though we were divine beings; they wait for us to guide them, even though they do not speak of it. And, too often, they look and wait in vain. Sometimes I think that the modern child is the loneliest child that ever lived. True, he has the radio and movies and television and amazing toys. True, he can belong to fine youth organizations and go to wonderful schools and take part in exciting sports. But the child who doesn't have the kind of parents who love him enough to teach him and inspire him is a child spiritually orphaned and emotionally starved; he is a victim of the modern parental crime of letting others do what should be a paramount responsibility of the father and mother. That is why I call him the loneliest child in the generations of mankind. And this loneliness also explains to a significant degree the alarming extent of juvenile maladjustment and delinquency today.

At the Midcentury White House Conference on Children and Youth, Dr. Lawrence Frank said that it takes four years of college, four years of Medical School, plus a year or two of internship, and then three or more years of specialized training to become a child psychiatrist who may or may not be able to help the child with his problem. But, it takes only the love, patience and understanding of parents to prevent the development of that problem.

Furthermore, I plead for a parenthood which takes the time to study the potentialities of the children. There are altogether too many boys and girls who graduate from high school and from college not knowing what they want to do. Our youth is in a desperate plight. Not only are they ignorant of what they desire to do, but also of what they are able to do. Yes, there are vocational counselors and guidance bureaus, and there are aptitude tests to be taken. Yet very few ever avail themselves of these facilities while the majority coast along from year to year with only a vague idea of what to do and with very little stimulus to do anything.

We may blame parents for a great deal of this indecision and confusion. Parents ought to make every effort to study the aptitudes of their children, to guide and direct these inclinations, to bring out latent abilities and to inspire them with the vision of living that kind of life which derives its happiness from contributing to the happiness of others. Parenthood is the greatest responsibility that God has ever given man because the child is the future. Every cradle shines with the light of the coming dawn; every infant is part of the promise of tomorrow's better world. In this very hour when delegates of the United Nations are meeting to solve the problems of the world, these leaders do not exercise greater power than do the humblest mother and father who, sensing their responsibilities to their children, are patiently and carefully and consistently shaping the form of the future as they shape the character and lifework of their young.

There is another responsibility which parents have toward their children and that is the responsibility of teaching the children, through precept and example, the dignity and beauty of family life, of marriage and the sanctity of morality. No one can view our present state of morals without being alarmed. The divorce rate is high and getting higher. Family life is weakened by the impact of our modern pleasure-mad world. Children are much too so-

phisticated for their years. There is so much that our
young people see and hear all around them which breaks
down their regard and reverence for the moral life.

Once again, I do not blame the children. I blame the
parents. No child should be allowed to grow up without
a religious education. When I say this I don't just mean
that a parent's responsibility ends upon sending the child
to Sunday School. The home must be religious; above
everything else the parents must be examples of religious
loyalty and faith. For the love of God is not so much
"taught" as it is "caught." When you sit down to your
table to eat with your children you ought to say grace, you
ought to return thanks to God for His bounties. And when
your children retire for the night and when they arise in
the morning, they should recite a prayer to our Heavenly
Father. The beautiful disciplines of religion should be followed in your homes with at least the avidity and interest
with which you follow the daily comic strips in your newspapers. You wouldn't miss reading the comics for anything. All that I ask is that you offer just that much
devoted homage to God. Read from the Bible to your
children. Let them become acquainted with the Psalms.
They may not understand every word and idea, but you
will explain these words and ideas. Thus, your conversation will turn to higher subjects, to loftier principles, to
ethics and morals, to what is right and what is wrong. Thus,
you will become teachers to your children and examples to
your children of all that constitutes the good life.

This same principle holds true for all the great spiritual
and moral ideals. If we want the future to be blessed with
a family life based on fidelity and trust and love, if we
want a future in which marriage is held sacred, and the
moral integrity of society is healthy and strong, then it

is up to the parents, right now, to influence their children, who will be that future, through proper guidance and, more than anything else, through noble example. The example of a good marriage enjoyed by one's father and mother usually prepares the child for such a blessed relationship in his own marriage. The same holds true for morality and intellectual and cultural interests; indeed, for all those virtues which make life worth living. Sometimes a good home produces a child who is bad, but this is an exception. "That the apple does not fall far from the tree" is an old saying which is constantly being verified by daily experience.

As perhaps never before, we need a happy, wholesome home life for our children, simply because the temptations and forces which undermine morality and religious belief are greater than ever. Our contemporary literature for the most part—the best sellers—usually consists of chronicles of immorality. The heroes and heroines are either Don Juans, Cleopatras, Jezebels, or Caesars. As for the motion pictures, I refer you to the lurid advertisements which depict beauteous sirens and herculean Casanovas breaking every known code, all for the thrills of love. Their arrival is emblazoned in glowing neon lights on the flashing marquees of your neighborhood theater every week. As for the radio and television programs which urge our youngsters to eat all the cereals so that they can be as strong as Super Duper Joe, the stories of adventure they enact to which our children listen so avidly, are scarcely more useful in the long run than the soap operas describing poor misunderstood wife and her dear silly blind husband who is, at best, either neglecting his home by spending too many hours at the office, or at worst, is involved with that sinister other woman.

Wherever we turn, we seem to find an environment which is almost overpoweringly hostile, either directly or indirectly, to those simple standards of virtue, beauty, learning and culture, faithfulness and moral idealism. Unless our children are fortified by parental precept and example in the home, then they must succumb to the blandishments of the outside world. Small wonder then that we are troubled about what the future holds in store for us when never was the benign force of the home so weak and the evil temptations outside so strong. It is an old maxim of psychologists that where you have a problem child you have a problem parent. This means that if we want a better, cleaner, finer life for all, then that desired future must be created through an inspired parent-child relationship in the immediate present. To neglect our children is to neglect and to reject our major responsibilities toward the future. For such tragic neglect the punishment is grim.

Up in the northern part of Sweden, a father and mother and two children went out one afternoon to pick berries. The parents became so busily engaged that they forgot to keep an eye on the children. When they were ready to go home they discovered to their dismay that the children had wandered off and were nowhere to be seen. They rushed frantically around looking and calling everywhere, but in vain. This continued for some hours, but still they were unable to find the children. The night had come and it was bitterly cold. Finally, the father suggested that they join hands and move together over the rocky terrain which they had traversed. In that way they would be sure to cover every inch of the land. This they did and they finally discovered the children, but by then it was too late. Too many precious hours had passed and the children were frozen to death.

Because of parental neglect the children perished. Let parents resolve to give more of themselves to their children, to learn to know their children so that they might be directed aright into the channels for which they show the greatest usefulness. They should join hands in love and faithfulness so that they may be examples of clean, inspiring moral living to their children. Let us do this, parents of America, before it is too late, before our children will be frozen to a spiritual death caused by parental indifference and neglect. Let the parents of America awaken to the crying need of the hour and be true mothers and fathers to their children so that our children may live and not die spiritually—so that our children who are the future may live in a world of faith and devotion, a world in which men will acknowledge, by the conduct of their lives, that their goal is the happiness of mature minds, the pleasure of healthy, clean bodies, the blessing of joyous homes, the satisfaction of humanitarian service to one's fellowmen and the abiding strength of trusting in the Lord.

CHAPTER X

The Saving Sense of Humor

ONCE I HAD the privilege of hearing the noted child psychologist, Dr. Frances Ilg, deliver a brilliant address entitled, "Why Children Act That Way." Her approach to, and her development of, her theme captivated the audience. Later on, as I thought about it, I realized that Dr. Ilg was able to impress us as she did primarily because her attitude toward her subject was governed by a delightful sense of humor. Possessing mastery of her theme, for she is a world-acknowledged authority in her field, she maintained a harmonious appreciation for parents and children alike. She was neither angry at the parents for their mistakes, nor was she provoked by the children for their contrary behavior. Indeed, one of the major points she made, throughout her lecture, was that parents ought to have, and should cultivate, a sense of humor in dealing with their children. I am sure that those of you who are parents will agree that we could all do much better in our homes, if we used the saving sense of humor, not only while rearing our children, but also in solving our own problems.

The more I think about the saving sense of humor, the more I am convinced that it would benefit all of us, in these turbulent times, were we to laugh a little bit more instead of becoming so enraged when we read about world problems and when we get into a political discussion.

To be sure we must be earnest and we must think our problems through, and we must not be frivolous about them. Each one of us should be reading and thinking and discussing the issues of our time, and searching for as much of the truth as we can obtain. But this earnest approach to the solution of our multifarious problems, this deep inquiry into the source of our troubles, need not be without the saving sense of humor. Whenever I think of someone who would be most likely to try to solve world problems with a set face, with a hard countenance, without even a glimmer of a smile, the picture that comes to my mind is that of Malik when he was the Chief Delegate of the Soviet Union to the United Nations. Many of us saw him in the cinema news or on television or in the newspapers. The man never smiled and he never relaxed. His appearance was like ice—hard, frozen, forbidding.

If I may generalize, and to generalize is always hazardous, I would say that, in essence, the Communist approach to the solution of the problems of life is characterized by the lack of a sense of humor. Now, when I think of a national characteristic of most Americans, of the typical American, I like to think of a human being with a friendly smile, with laughter in his heart; of a person who is blessed with a generous portion of the saving sense of humor. I like to think of Abraham Lincoln whose sense of humor often saved him from being overwhelmed by life's tragedies and, as he approached his crucial problems, provided him with that inner strength which enabled him to persevere and win.

However, during the most recent presidential campaigns, more of us acted like Malik than Lincoln. At dinner meetings, or luncheon meetings, or in somebody's parlor, one could not deal with the presidential election without the passion temperature going up, voices getting tense, strident, and a violent intolerance on the part of the speaker for anybody's point of view except his own. Anger was running too fast and too high, and I don't think it did any of us any good. When we are angry, we lose control. When our tempers are aroused, we say things which we regret in a calmer mood. It would be far better for all of us if we could hold on, as Lincoln did, to a sense of humor, which is to say to hold on to a broad, balanced perspective of ourselves and of our problems.

Consider the significance of the saving sense of humor in dealing with our private, domestic affairs. In every home, there are problems. Being human, we will differ with one another, no matter how much we love one another. If we were to imagine that the only happy marriage is the marriage in which there are no problems, no differences, no disagreements—we would imagine an impossibility. Marital and family happiness does not mean the absence of disagreements between husband and wife, parents and children. It is impossible to have a relationship like marriage with no one presenting an opposing thought, nor doing anything which displeases. Problems and disagreements are bound to arise. But the husband and wife who are really in love manage to solve these problems amicably, sensibly, and co-operatively. They learn to respect one another's differences—yes, even one another's idiosyncrasies and peculiarities. And one of the most effective ways to develop this respect, as Dr. Ilg tells us, is to have a saving sense of humor, and use that sense for all it is worth.

The saving sense of humor which I recommend is very remote from the laughter we enjoy when we listen to comedians, or watch a funny show on the stage or screen or television. It is related to this, of course, but very distantly. For the saving sense of humor which we need so much today is actually rooted in the sense of compassion and pity, of empathy, sympathy and a profound awareness of the tragedy in life. It is also based upon a sense of humility.

Have you ever watched a little child first learning how to walk? See him, how he first takes hold of the side of a chair and pulls himself up, and stands there at last, swaying a bit, very uncertain. Then he looks up at you, with your arms outstretched to him as you wait to see him take his first two or three steps all on his own. With all the faith, and the love, and the courage in the world, the little child takes a step forward, and can almost take a second when he collapses and falls down. But only for a moment, for he tries again and again. And when at last he falls triumphantly into your arms, it is hard to tell who is prouder, the child or you, over the achievement of this supreme victory. But there is one thing which always happens when that child falls into your arms—both of you laugh! And it is the laughter of the angels—of deepest joy and blessing. It is the laughter of pride and love. It is the laughter of perfect happiness.

Now it is possible to watch the struggles of a child learning how to walk, and just stand there and roar with laughter at the way he staggers and sways and falls. You can watch and laugh *at* him. If you do this, you are, in essence, regarding him as an object of ridicule; and what he is doing is amusing you, as you look down upon him from your adult position of superiority. You can stand there, upon your own feet, but he, groping and uncertain and inadequate, falls down again and again. There is a world of difference between laughing *at* the child, and laughing *with* him as he masters the art of walking. Surely, there is no semblance whatsoever between the laughter of ridicule and the laughter of sympathy and love. And what we need so much today is the laughter based upon sympathy and love which grows out of what Micah called, "Walking humbly with thy God."

If you don't have this saving sense of humor, and would like to begin to develop it, then the most important place to begin is to learn to laugh at yourself. Maybe you think this is very easy, but we find in our contact with people and in our studies of people, that this is possibly the hardest thing in the world to do. Oh, it is nothing at all to laugh at others. You know so-called "practical jokers," who love to do things to make other people look ridiculous—but just try to play a practical joke on a "practical joker," and see whether he will laugh at himself. Usually, he gets furious, and angry, and he sulks. "The idea of anyone making a monkey out of me!" he mutters to himself. Maybe one of the reasons why it is so hard to learn to laugh at ourselves is that we like to think of ourselves as perfect—as being unable to make a mistake—as doing everything we undertake to do, faultlessly.

Consider this domestic situation: The husband has graciously offered to carry the empty soft-drink bottles out to the garage. He piles one upon another in a tremendous heap and is about to set forth upon his mission. His wife admonishes him, "But, darling, you can't carry all those bottles—there are far too many—you will drop them!" "Oh, no!" says our positive Sir Galahad and boastful Hercules. "It's nothing at all for me to carry as many as this! Why, I am sure I could carry twice as many! Just watch me!" Well, you know what happens. His wife watches him. Crash! The bottles are broken! He stands there roaring with rage. He blames his wife for asking him to take the bottles out in the first place—he blames his children for drinking too much—he blames his wife for buying so much—he blames everyone, all over the landscape, except himself. And the very last thing that such a man would do is to laugh at himself, which he ought to do, for in essence it is a very funny situation.

In that very popular book, "The Caine Mutiny," by Herman Wouk, we meet with a monstrous character, Lt. Commander Phillip Queeg, who makes life impossible for his officers and crew. He was a veritable sadist in the way he inflicted punishment upon his men over trifles, which went so far as to cause the nervous breakdown of one of them. If you have read this story, you will recall that Queeg had no sense of humor. He had no humility, nor compassion, nor sympathy. He was the kind of man who had to be right, regardless—who found as his only source of laughter the humiliation of his subordinates, who delighted in cracking the whip of authority. The basic reason for this absorbing book's deserved popularity, I think, is that it deals with a character who is, alas, much too common. We find Queegs everywhere. We find him in domineering husbands, humorless fathers, demanding wives, insolent children and in business and government. We find a Queeg wherever we encounter people who are hard-hearted and cruel. And none of these Queegs has a sense of humor, except that harsh variety which rejoices in another person's downfall. They certainly are unable to laugh at themselves, and they bring sorrow and misery into our world.

The medical profession advises us that laughter is good for one's health. The body relaxes when we laugh, and it tightens up when we are angry. I wonder if it has occurred to you, as it has to me, that the sound of "laugh" and "love" are very close to one another? Love and laugh go together. As Bennett Cerf once said, "Very few people get into serious trouble when they are laughing." Anger and hate poison the system of the human being. They lead to a variety of fatal ailments. Many a controversy in this world which ends disastrously might have been saved by laughter. Laughter breaks the ice of aloofness in a social gathering. Laughter breaks down the walls that separate people. When you can laugh together, you can work together. Laughter heals the body and the soul. We don't begin to live until we have developed a sense of humor which clears away the stormy clouds, and lets the sunlight come in.

The great Carlyle once said, "The man who cannot laugh is not only fit for treasons, stratagems and spoils, but his whole life is already a treason and a stratagem." But let me emphasize the point that this has nothing to do with ridicule and "practical jokes," nor laughter at someone else's expense. In the book, "Spark of Life," by Erich Remarque, is recorded the overwhelming tragedy of what happened to the victims of a concentration camp, in the closing days of the defeat of Germany. The most terrible episodes are those in which the Nazis laugh at the outcries of helpless prisoners who are being tortured. Such laughter, of course, is diseased, morbid, pathological.

We Americans, in these hectic days of domestic and international political controversy, are having our sense of humor severely tested. Now is the time, if ever, when we ought to deal with one another with a quality of mercy and brotherhood, of tolerance and sympathy, which will enable us to go forward after domestic elections and United Nations decisions without having caused those

THE SAVING SENSE OF HUMOR

wounds which time can never heal. To do this, we must develop the right perspective. We ought to see ourselves, not as members of conflicting parties, but as citizens of "One nation, indivisible, with liberty and justice for all," and as part of humanity. The moment we forget the larger picture, the moment we stop realizing that there is a tomorrow to be lived, a future to be realized, in which this world will go on, our country will go on, we become bigoted and mentally congested.

Granted, that it is important for us to get all the facts we can, and take our sides and strive earnestly for the election of those whom we regard to be best suited to assume the responsibilities of governmental position. Granted, that there is nothing more important for us than to choose sides, and to vote, and to think seriously about everything pertaining to what goes on in Washington, in our State and local legislatures, in the United Nations and in our foreign policy! Nevertheless, no amount of earnestness and seriousness in this area of meeting adequately our citizen's responsibilities should make us lose our sense of humor. To achieve this delicate and fine balance of devotion to one's own point of view, and the higher devotion to the unity which is America, as well as our duties to humanity, requires the saving sense of humor. This means that we will always remember that the other party is not all wrong, and we are not all right, and that this country will not go to the dogs if one major party comes into office and the other major party is defeated. A saving sense of humor will remind us that the American people are not going to deliberately surrender their dignity and their liberty and that humanity at large yearns to be free.

There is a wonderful sentence in the Book of Proverbs, in Chapter 31, which describes the "Woman of Valor."

Beginning with the tenth verse, we have in that chapter the world-renowned description of the ideal woman. It could just as well be the description of the ideal man—the ideal human being. You will recall that in this section the Bible describes the diligence, the seriousness, the industriousness of the "Woman of Valor." She carries on her household duties and is never idle. She accepts and fulfills her responsibilities magnificently. And then we come upon this sentence: "Strength and dignity are her clothing, and she laugheth at the time to come."

Of course she laugheth at the time to come, for she is a person who has a sense of humor, a confidence born out of her own innate spiritual worth. Indeed, the very next verse, following the one I just quoted, upholds the main thought of our discussion, for thus reads the 26th verse: "She openeth her mouth with wisdom: and the law of kindness is on her tongue." I submit, that for you and for me, for all Americans in this crucial time—there is nothing better for us to do, as we go about the sacred task of keeping America "the land of the free, and the home of the brave," than to invoke upon our tongues the law of kindness—and that we clothe ourselves with strength and dignity—and speak the words of healing and wisdom. If we do these things, we can live our lives joyously, for we will never forget that we are privileged to live in a glorious country, the leader of the free world. We will then look upon our fellow Americans and fellowmen everywhere with proper perspective, guided by the laws of brotherhood, and the saving sense of humor. Thus shall we, too, be able to laugh at the time to come, because, strengthened by the modesty of being able to laugh at ourselves, upheld by the confidence which faces the future unafraid, sustained by a deep humility and faith in God, we shall know that we are bound to come through victoriously. We can then believe, with all of our hearts and souls, that happiness is our destiny.

But what keeps us from possessing this buoyant belief and prevents us from developing the saving sense of humor? Why won't we, perversely enough, do the things which can fill our lives with happiness?

At the end of Chapter One we observed that, frequently, we ourselves are the main obstacle in the path which leads to the enjoyment of living. It is time that we took a closer look at the "Self."

CHAPTER XI

The Self

DURING a conversation with a friend whom I consider a great teacher, I asked him what he thought was the most important subject to discuss with youth and adults alike in these challenging days. He replied that he would speak on the importance of the "Self." He said that he would use, as the basis of his message, the world-renowned concluding words of advice by Polonius to his son in Shakespeare's "Hamlet"; "This, above all; to thine own self be true, and it must follow as the night the day, thou canst not then be false to any man."

It may seem strange that I, who am a religious teacher, should stress the importance of regard for one's "Self." On first sight, you might believe that I am advocating selfishness, when all of us are much more accustomed to hearing the Self attacked as a cause of misery and sorrow in the world. Indeed, selfishness is a major source of trouble, but not all self-concern is evil. Self-confidence and self-respect, for example, are virtues. To have faith in yourself is an absolute imperative if you are to find life worth living for yourself, as well as to make it worth living for others. The Bible is very specific about this point. In Leviticus, Chapter 19, verse 18, we read, "Thou shalt love thy neighbor as thyself." In these words the Bible tells you and me that it is expected that we love ourselves; its call to us to love others is based on the love of one's self. Modern scientific research in the psychology of human relations supports this ancient maxim of the Bible, for we know that a person who hates himself cannot love others.

Not only is the moral teaching of the Bible based on the proper love of self, but also the entire American faith in freedom is based upon this concept. For the very essence of the American tradition is faith in the individual, love for the individual, belief in the individual's power to work out his destiny. This faith was beautifully and proudly expressed for all of us by Thomas Jefferson, when he wrote in the immortal Declaration of Independence, "We hold these truths to be self-evident, that all men are created equal, and are endowed by their Creator with certain inalienable Rights, that among these are Life, Liberty and the pursuit of Happiness."

As far as the United States is concerned, these ideals establish, for all time, our faith in the human being, our emphasis upon human rights above all other rights. Thus, the weight of American history is on the side of the individual, rather than the government. The government is established to help the individual. The State exists for the benefit of man—not man for the benefit of the State. The Constitution of the country is sacred, but far more sacred are the rights of man, so that the Constitution carries within itself provisions for amendments, for changes in order to meet the changing needs of the individual citizens who make up the nation. Even so, the laws of the land are sacred, but far more holy is the right of the people to change these laws when they no longer satisfy the highest interests of the people.

Similarly, the elected officials of the nation occupy a sacred office, but they, too, are only servants of the people, they are representatives of the people, and can be brought in or turned out of office according to the votes of the people. It cannot be stressed too often, or too much, that what is unique and thrilling about our American way of life is the sanctity of the individual. And this sanctity and dignity and authority of the individual is based upon the belief that God created the individual. Because of your divine origin, and mine, we have been endowed by our Creator with certain rights; and to the protection and maintenance and realization of these rights are our representatives in government presumably dedicated.

It is a great pity that not enough of us are aware of the significance of the part which the Judaeo-Christian religious tradition has played in creating the foundations of our Democracy. It is a pity because our failure to recognize this has made not only for widespread paganism and secularism in our conduct, but also it has opened the way to the breakdown of the supreme American tradition which is faith in the individual. The moment you forget that your self is of sacred origin, that very moment you have opened the door to Fascism and Communism. When people surrender their faith in the divine origin of self, they surrender their innate rights to "Life, Liberty, and the pursuit of Happiness."

This surrender has come about through a number of powerful influences. The first influence, I think, is the rejection of God. This rejection alienates the mind from the profoundest historical tradition of the Western World. Only this tradition of faith in God has provided the lowliest individual with his claim to dignity. As long as we believe that we are God's children, we cannot but oppose man's inhumanity to man. It was precisely this faith which enabled the founding fathers of this country to proclaim,

"Resistance to tyranny is obedience to God." It goes without saying, of course, that the rejection of God launches us out upon a way of life which is essentially immoral, unethical, and swollen with unbridled greed. Only as we come back to a genuine faith in God do we return to a genuine faith in man, who is the child of God. It is no accident that the founding fathers of our Democracy were God-revering men, whereas the founders and followers of Communism were, and are, God-hating men.

The second influence which has undermined the proper regard for the self is a false evaluation of the findings of science. Science has taught us how to prolong life and how to make the chores of life easier to accomplish and has relieved us of so many of the burdens of what would otherwise be enslaving tasks. But science has also created the Atom Bomb, the Warplane, the Battleship and all of the cunning implementations of the force of destruction. The mistake we make is to worship science as an end in itself instead of regarding it as a wonderful tool and instrument. We have forgotten that science asks "how?" not "why?"—"what?" not "where?" Science itself is a neutral instrument which, for its final value, depends on the use to which it is put by man. Place a gun, which is a scientific invention, in the hands of an evil man and with it he will murder his fellowman. It will increase the potency and scope of his criminality. Put that same gun in the hands of a good man and he will use it to preserve law and order, to kill dangerous wild animals, to add to the safety and the happiness of life. The gun itself, you see, is neutral. Thus, atomic energy is neutral—thus, science is neutral. Whether or not science is good or bad depends upon the uses to which it is put by human beings. I disagree heartily with those people who look upon science as the enemy of religion—I only see irreligious people making science a source of conflict, instead of a source of blessing to all humanity. Nevertheless, the fact remains that many have forsaken religion and made science their god and thus they have lost the proper faith in the self.

There is another influence which has destroyed faith in the self and that is the wrong conclusions which people have made on the basis of the findings of psychology, psychiatry, and psychoanalysis. Instead of realizing that these findings are remarkable approaches toward the attainment of mental health, so many of us fix our attention upon the morbid revelations which have left us utterly dismayed. For example, psychiatry has discovered that much of the mental illness of adult life finds its origin in the unfortunate experiences of childhood. Whereupon, in a very shallow and superficial manner, many jump to the conclusion that families are no good, and parents are no good, and that fathers and mothers are far more of an evil than they are a blessing. What a ridiculous, illogical conclusion! It seems to me that the reasonable conclusion is that these findings of psychiatry alert all parents to the supreme importance of their role in the lives of their children and thus help to make all of us wiser and better parents in our relationship with our children.

We should feel grateful to the students and physicians of the mind for supporting the teachings of our religious heritage, which emphasize the sanctity of the home and the crucial responsibilities of parents in the home, as well as the sanctity of marriage itself. We should rejoice to find psychiatrists corroborating the ancient insight of religion, that no matter how a person may have fallen away from the right path, he can come back again, he can return, he can change for the better. Long ago, it was said, "A little knowledge is a dangerous thing." And I, for one, am convinced that it is the little knowledge that most of us have about the real meaning of the findings of psychology which has led us astray.

Let me tell you what I, a religious teacher, see in people. Wherever I turn in this world today, I find the evidences of the greatness and the nobility of the self. I know that there is much evil in the world, much cruelty, but I believe that, by and large, the human being everywhere is, or yearns to be, on the side of righteousness. I am far from ready to consign the human race to oblivion on the premise that it deserves such a dire fate. And certainly, here in our own country, we should be the last people in the world to lose faith in the dignity of the self of every individual. To lose this faith is to lose the America we love. In connection with this point, let us remind ourselves what a mistake it is, in the long run, to blame all our problems on one man in the White House; and on the other hand to fondly anticipate that the arrival of another man there will solve all our difficulties. To think, and to act, like this is to run contrary to the American tradition and to religious tradition. The reason for this is that, in essence, such an attitude marks the abdication of an individual from his own rights and responsibilities. America is not one particular political party. It is the people—it is every individual, every citizen. The salvation of our country does not depend upon one person or group of persons. It depends upon *you* and *me*—upon every citizen. We could not so easily relinquish our own responsibilities to others without first surrendering the proper regard for the self. I don't think we could hate as intensely as we do if we respected the divine origin of every one of us, regardless of creed and color.

As Shakespeare said, "To thine own self be true, and it must follow as the night the day, thou canst not then be false to any man." The implication here is that your self is innately good—that the "you" which is really you, is something noble, something which is spiritually great. This must be what Shakespeare had in mind, or he could not have followed the instruction to be true to the self by claiming that by so doing you could not then be false to anybody.

I wonder if you have met people, as I have, who try so hard to give you the impression that they are not fine, that they are not good; but rather that they are shrewd and conniving and terribly daring. How we pose before one another! How we try to act tough and aggressive, and self-sufficient! We seem to be masters at giving a false impression of ourselves. Conversely, many of us act inferior and weak and cowardly. We seem to have convinced ourselves that we are not strong—we have no courage—we have no innate goodness. But the truth is neither that we are so bad and strong, nor that we are so inferior and weak. The truth is that we have not begun to develop our own spiritual resources, we have not begun to give the self the chance to express its own pure, honest nature. Believing that God has made us, we must believe that a God of love and goodness has made us in His spiritual image. A diseased man, a sick soul, a perverted human being may find delight in evil, may love to do evil, but these are the exceptions who only prove the rule that most of us are only happy, are only truly content, when we are doing those things which bring happiness to others.

I am very fond of an old story which goes like this: After Adam and Eve had sinned and thereby lost their claim to divinity, God caused a deep sleep to fall upon them. He called a council of the angels and God said to the Heavenly Hosts, "When Adam and Eve awaken, they will know that they are no longer divine, that they have lost their divine powers and they will go in search of their divinity. Tell Me, My angels, where shall I conceal this divinity so that they shall not be able to find it?" And one of the angels spoke up and said, "Lord of the Universe, let us conceal their divinity within themselves for that is the last place that they will go in search of it."

How brilliantly does this story illuminate the triumph and the tragedy of the human being. You and I do have divinity within ourselves. We are the children of God. And yet, we do not seek divine glory within the self but rather do we try to find it everywhere else. Sometimes we think that we shall be like gods if we are only wise enough, and so we pursue knowledge, we worship science eagerly and slavishly, but we do not find it there. Sometimes we think that we shall be divine if we have power in wealth or in station. But this cannot satisfy the human heart, the inner need, the deep pain. And then we go off wildly in the direction of political power, and whether we be a Herod or Caesar, a Napoleon, a Hitler or a Stalin, or any of the lesser known variety of demagogue-dictator, we think that we have realized divine attainments. But the evil pride of man only leads him to his doom and he walks alone and finally brings about untimely death and widespread destruction.

It is high time that we turned from our vain and futile search for divinity in every place except where it may be found. It is time that we understood that God has placed within every human being His divine glory. You have it! And I have it! As the old spiritual expresses it, "All God's children got wings." Yes, we all have wings. If only we would fly. If only we would rise spiritually by recognizing our innate goodness, and live accordingly.

Unfortunately, a powerful barrier to this desirable flight of the spirit can be the environment in which we are born and live. We recognize the importance of heredity or nature as a background for our physical and mental progress. But what about nurture or environment? How much of a part does environment play in molding the self of each individual?

CHAPTER XII

The Power of Environment

THE GREAT Greek philosopher, Socrates, used to say on numerous occasions, "Know thyself."

That it is most important to have self-knowledge, to understand our own capacities, ought to be self-evident. In the process of growing up we test our aptitudes, our talents, our abilities, and it is assumed that by the time we reach adulthood we know ourselves enough to choose a way of life in which we can live successfully and joyfully. Unfortunately, life reveals too many square pegs in round holes and vice versa; too many people who are not doing what they would like to do and who, as a consequence, are very unhappy human beings. How do we get to be the way we are?

There are a number of factors which go into making us the kind of persons we are. I want to discuss a major factor, namely, the power of environment. Surely no one can analyze accurately why he is what he is and thinks as he does, if he overlooks the influence of environment. Our prejudices, opinions, our points of view, attitudes, politics, religion, likes and dislikes, ideals and morals, our national pride, our world outlook, all of these are in large measure controlled by environmental conditions.

It is always amusing to meet a person who lives with the remarkable conceit that whatever he thinks and does is due to his own choice and a self-determined course of action. I have never forgotten a conversation I had on this subject with the late Clarence Darrow. He pointed out how important is the factor of chance in our lives, especially insofar as it produces the environment in which we live. It is, of course, chance that makes us born male or female, sick or healthy, rich or poor. It is chance that makes us appear on this earth, either in China or India or the United States or England, or wherever we are born. We ourselves didn't choose to be Jews or Catholics or Protestants, or whatever our faith may be. We are born into our nationality, into our color, into our religion. Moreover, it is chance alone which determines whether we are born into a home which is sound or unsound, which is helpful or injurious to our healthy development. The environment, then, into which we come as infants is not of our choice. We just find ourselves where we are. This discourse on chance by Darrow made a great impression upon me. Now let us carry our discussion on the power of environment to another area.

From the great light which now is being focused by psychologists and psychiatrists on childhood, we have come to realize that so many of our problems as adults, if not all of them, go back to our childhood. It was one of the great discoveries of Freud that a neurotic person is one who suffers from unresolved emotional conflicts of childhood. Such an individual cannot ever grow beyond this conflict until he comes to terms with that problem and understands it and, if possible, solves it entirely. Freud's method of cure, you will remember, was to have the patient talk out his life, revive the memory of the repressed and long-forgotten shock experience. I do not know of any competent authority in the field who denies this insight and all seem to be unanimous in stressing the point that the unresolved emotional conflicts or trauma of childhood remain as a festering element which may later take the form of a serious emotional upset, or of a sense of insecurity, throughout life. With this added insight it seems quite clear that a large part of what we are and what we do and how we feel is not of our own immediate choosing but rather is due to the accumulated influence of our general and personal environment upon us.

Consider, too, the sectional prejudices which we inherit, so to speak, through the environment in which we are born and live. If you live in Texas, you have certain attitudes with regard to your State, in relationship to other states, which are so pronounced that you have practically an international reputation for boasting about your part of the country. If you live in a very large city, you have attitudes toward the man who lives in the country. Similarly, the man in the country has prejudices with regard to the city folk. Being born in one part of the United States often puts you into one of the political parties.

I remember a man who told me that he and his father and grandfather before him had lived in the South. Moreover, he assured me that in every election he gave each issue confronting the electorate and every candidate running for office the most careful scrutiny and investigation. Then he concluded by saying, "And thank God, every time I have managed to come out voting for the Democratic Party." My friend was only deceiving himself, of course. The power of his environment has molded him as it molds most of us.

It is important to observe how the forces which shape our lives outside of the home, namely the school and the church, as well as the newspaper and radio and movies and television and advertisements, overwhelm us by the omnipotence of their influence. We tend to take on the whole mental aspect and physical phase of our environment. We dress a certain way and we eat a particular way and we observe certain customs, and we speak with accents or drawls primarily because of the nature of behavior in the place we live. Obviously, none of us was born to believe that we must rise and start singing when they play "The Eyes of Texas are upon You." We are not born, for example, an American, or an Englishman, or a German, or a Russian. We are born just impressionable human beings who are conditioned by our environment to be American or English or French, or whatever be our nationality, and we are trained to stand up at the sound of our National Anthem. Even the styles of clothes we wear, the kind of automobiles we drive, the books we read, the radio programs we listen to, these are brought into our lives through the power of propaganda, through the influence of advertisement, through the subtle, the indirect pressures of the locale in which we live.

Why is it so important for us to recognize the power of environment? Well, for a number of reasons. To begin with, it ought to make us humble. It ought to make us less positive about how almighty righteous we are and how entirely wrong the next fellow may be. To be so positive about the righteousness of our side and the wrongness of the other side seems ridiculous when we face the facts of the power of environment. How can you be so certain that what you believe is true when your convictions probably come not from your own careful thoughts and decisions, but rather from your uncritical acceptance of the environment in which you live! Surely, many conflicts would never have taken place, many quarrels would never have ensued if more people were conscious of the real origin of their pet ideas, phobias and attitudes. For I don't see how it is possible for any human being to escape conditioning by the society in which he lives. It is bound to occur. It is inevitable. If we happen to be born in an Italy which glories in Caesar, we too will dream dreams of imperial glory. If we happen to be living in Germany when a Hitler is in power, we will parrot his hates and his violence. If we are born in the United States we will accept as our God-given right the privilege to vote, to criticize our government, to assemble freely, to worship freely, to expect to live in freedom and in liberty always.

It is possible, you see, to condition people toward becoming saints or devils, freedom-loving citizens or totalitarian slaves. The book by the late George Orwell called "1984" is a terrifying prophecy of a world which is completely under the tyrannical power of dictators. It is a shocking picture that he describes in which no one can see the truth, know the facts, can love or marry or have children without being under the engulfing influence of the Police State. The most terrible thing about this book is that it only carries through to their awful, logical conclusions what we have already seen begun in our lifetime in many parts of the world. The difference between people living in a totalitarian State and those living in a free State is due essentially to environmental influence.

Once we recognize the power of environment upon us, we have already taken a step in the direction of being critical, of choosing, of examining, of discriminating between one influence and another. We begin to understand how important it is to provide all of the people with the best kind of education, the best kind of opportunities. We then recognize that all of us are responsible for one another, that we are part of an organic society, that we are our brother's keeper, that there is social responsibility for individual happiness or misery, good or evil. By accepting environmental conditioning as a phenomenon which acts upon every human being, we become merciful and compassionate toward the weaknesses of others. We do not condemn so quickly. If our neighbor does something that we don't like, if we confront a form of behavior which offends us, we will not hate or reject but we will recognize that the offensive act or the offending neighbor is the end result of certain influences which can be changed. And then it is up to us to provide him with those experiences and influences which will produce in him those qualities which are favorable to co-operative human relationships.

We can, at last, come to realize, in appraising the power of environment, that no human being is lost completely, no one is bad beyond redemption, no one is to be hated and despised. A person has either had the opportunity to grow or his growth has been stunted. He has either been taught to walk in the ways of righteousness or he has been misled by his experiences. Completely discredited are all the old-fashioned ideas that certain traits are in the blood, that Germans must plunge the world into war, that East is East and West is West and never the twain shall meet, that there is no hope for any human being or group who constitute a source of danger or who are hostile to the welfare of the whole. We are, at last, coming to understand that our world is what we make it, that we must contribute to the advance of our society, that stability is impossible for one nation if it is not enjoyed by all.

How invigorating it is to find that the great insights which are being given to us by science today agree with the vision of religion which so long ago maintained with the prophet Malachi, "Have we not all one Father, hath not one God created us?"

Some time ago, I had the pleasure of seeing three prominent men of my city honored by the Vice-President of the United States. It was a genuine restoration of the soul to have been part of that vast throng of men and women who gathered to pay tribute to their brethren who had achieved something which we now recognize to be the most valuable goal of all. These men were not honored because of their material laurels or because they were successful merchants or successful candidates for office. They were not being honored for anything that they had obtained for themselves. The reason for the tribute given to them was because of their service to others, to humanity. The National Conference of Christians and Jews gave to these men Certificates of Distinction in Human Service —in Interfaith Relationships. These men, as they rose to receive the honor, heard themselves eulogized by friends. And what was it that ran as a theme throughout all of these eulogies? It was that these men regarded themselves to be their brothers' keeper, that they never made any distinction between rich or poor, between color or creed, that they gave themselves to others and thereby poured into the environmental stream of life the conditioning influence of love, the indoctrination of a noble example, of lifting up their fellowmen.

For us who were present that night there was the feeling that nothing was more important for the survival of the human race, in these critical years, than that more and more people should undertake to make their contribution to the advance and progress of their community. Obviously, there could be no war in a world where people took into account the welfare of others. War is waged by that kind of mind which sees and profits from seeing the human race as divided, segmented, fragmentized. Wholeness and peace and happiness come into the world through the agency of those whose lives are founded on the belief that as our Father is One in Heaven, so are we one upon earth.

Let us understand, then, the mighty role that all of us play in the lives of one another. Let us appreciate the power of environment. Let us be humble about our own achievements and compassionate in measuring the shortcomings of others. There was once a Bishop who, seeing a criminal being led to the gallows, said to a fellow Bishop, "There but for the grace of God, go I." Thus he recognized the power of environment to make or break a man.

Using the insight of the Bishop for our own needs today, we may say to ourselves and to all the people of the world, "Ahead of us lies chaos, confusion and destruction if we turn aside from our social obligations, if we refuse to accept our individual role and responsibility in hastening the coming of the Golden Age. Darkness and confusion will surely come to us if we reject the grace of God. But we can also accept God's grace and ahead of us, as a consequence, can be an age of great enlightenment, a magnificent environment into which every human being is born, an environment fertile for the growth of the spirit, flooded with the sunshine of understanding and compassion. Yes, there lies ahead of us a promised world toward which all of us can go by working together, thoughtful of one another, remembering that as man rises God rises. As we create the environment of peace by our own words and deeds of pacifism we shall establish, at last, a world at peace; a world of co-operation in which, as the Bible prophesied, "Every man shall dwell under his vine and fig tree and none shall make him afraid."

Nevertheless, that promised world of earthly peace upheld by men of good-will remains nebulous and unborn. Another tremendous block to the realization of that better world is involved in the conflict which rages in the minds of men with regard to what is true. Let us explore this most perplexing, yet fascinating, question.

CHAPTER XIII

The Search for Truth

WHAT IS the process by which we come to the conclusion that this or that statement or opinion is true, whereas the other statement, the other claim, is not true? It is important for us to know this because in the search for truth, you and I are involved in the most significant quest of our lives.

Of all creatures that live, the human being is the only one that will die for the sake of what he regards to be true. The whole history of religious and political martyrdom is the story of valiant men and women who willingly sacrificed themselves, who even joyfully died, for what they held to be the truth. Whether it be Socrates, drinking the hemlock poison, a martyr in behalf of the free mind; or Rabbi Akiba, tortured and burned to death by the same Roman imperialism and paganism which crucified Jesus, and exclaiming as he died, "God is one"; or the four Army chaplains, Rev. Clark V. Poling, Rev. George L. Cox, Father John Patrick Washington and Rabbi Alexander D. Goode, their hands joined and praying together as they went down on the transport *S. S. Dorchester* in wintry seas, early in 1942, having given their life preservers away so that others might survive—these immortals of former days, as well as the intrepid of our own time, are an illustrious testament to that unique virtue of mankind which for the sake of what is held to be true will courageously live and die.

Let us state, here at the outset of our consideration of the subject of truth, that we are fully aware of the hazards and difficulties involved in the pursuit of our theme. He is bold, indeed, who would venture further on the stormy seas of inquiry into this subject. This is daring because all the peoples of the world are in a turbulence of discord with regard to what is true. Even a momentary consideration of our subject makes it very clear that what is true for some people is not held to be true by others. All of us have certain doctrines to which we cling tenaciously and which we would defend with all of our means and with life itself against those who would destroy our tenets.

We know that in the world of politics, and in the philosophy of government, we Americans of democratic faith repudiate the truths of the Communist. They, in turn, call our ideals of government false and dangerous and destructive. We believe it to be true that the individual is supreme, whereas they maintain that the state is supreme. Remember how the Declaration of Independence uses the phrase, "We hold these *truths* to be self-evident," and then goes on to glorify the dignity of the individual and his right to "life, liberty, and the pursuit of happiness." At bottom then, the entire controversy between Communism and Democracy is a battle concerning that which is considered to be true and that which is considered to be false. Whether we recognize it or not, the future success of either one of these giant competitors for the mind of man depends on the extent to which the human race at large is persuaded and convinced that one or the other is true.

But, it is not alone in the field of politics and government that we are swept by conflicting testimony of what is true.

We also find in the religious realm, in the religious beliefs of mankind, doctrines which do not harmonize with one another, doctrines which separate and divide. To be sure, the faithful ones of a religious movement take it upon themselves to convert others to what they regard to be true in religious faith. Thus, we have missionaries and missionary organizations whose object is to convert. We find, among some major religions of the world, the doctrine that all those who do not believe as their particular group believes are forever lost and doomed to suffer throughout all eternity. I can tell you, from my own personal experience, that almost every day brings some letter in the mails urging me to turn from my false path, and accept the path of the true faith.

Not so long ago, a lady who is a devoted listener to my radio programs, came to call on me. She first told me how much she enjoyed my talks. And then, after the usual pleasantries had been exchanged, she launched upon her mission. She said to me, with tears in her eyes, "I am worried about the salvation of your soul. You do not worship the true God. You simply must come to understand that unless you accept the faith of my church, you are certainly going to end up in Hell." And she continued, "Each night, I pray for your soul and your salvation, and I beg of you to change at once before it is too late." Now, I did not argue with her, but I did thank her for her interest in me and my soul and I assured her that nothing could pain me more than to reflect upon the possibility of spending an eternity in the torrid regions of Hades. I told her that I would think about her mission to me and I would always be grateful for her friendly interest.

You may ask, why didn't I argue with the lady? Perhaps she is reading this now. I am sure she will be interested to learn what I have to say further upon her visit. The reason why I did not argue with her is because, first of all, I respect her convictions. She is obviously sincere in her belief and in her fears concerning my future. Nothing that I could possibly say to her would change her mind. Moreover, were I to tell her that I consider a religion to be very small when it crowds any human being out who does not agree; and were I to try to impress upon her the fact that since God is the father of all mankind and is a God of love, that it is incredible to me that God denies His love to any of His creatures as long as they try to reach Him—well, if I were to say this, she would probably look at me as though I were demented and speaking an unintelligible language. I refer to this instance only because it is a vivid illustration of the constant clash that goes on within our lives between what we regard to be true and what others hold to be the truth.

But this search for truth is not alone confined to government and religion. It is also present in our family life and in our personal lives. When folks get married, they want to enjoy the true marriage, to make their marriage successful. Each person in a marriage strives to be, in the beginning at least, an ideal kind of husband or wife. In the marriage ceremony we pledge our lives to one another, our everlasting love to one another. It is a very beautiful thing, this wedding ceremony, but so often marriage itself fails. The abysmal record of divorce in America tells the sad story of husbands and wives whose standards of what is expected of them in marriage differ so widely, who disappoint one another so greatly that they cannot possibly find happiness together and thus come to a parting of the ways. At heart, it is a conflict between standards and ideals. What is true for one is false for the other.

We find a similar situation of differences in parent-children relationships. Recognizing, as so many of us do, our deplorable inadequacy, we read books by child psychologists, we rush to lectures and we devour advice to parents on how to deal, for example, with that mysterious creature known as the adolescent. We are told that every child who goes wrong, every delinquent, is a tragic evidence of a father and mother who failed. And we who are the kind of parents who care about doing a good job as parents keep worrying about how to fulfill the true role of a father and a mother. For surely no normal parent wants to hurt a child and all normal parents mean well by their children. Thus, each one of us in our homes is confronted with the challenge of what we regard to be true, what we affirm as being valid responsibilities for us to meet as parents.

I do not believe that we have arrived at a consensus as yet. I don't think so because I have yet to encounter any kind of parental ruling, for example, on such things as when girls should start to wear formal clothes, when they should begin to go out on dates, and how late they should be permitted to stay when they do go out. To be sure, one finds rules, but they are different regulations. What is true for one house, is not necessarily true for the next. Very often, when I express my dismay to parents at the early age of dating and wearing formal clothes and staying out late, the response that I receive is, "Well, you just wait until your children grow up, wait until they get a little older and then we'll see what you can do about it." Now, regardless of the rightness or the wrongness of this situation, the point I want to make is that there would be no problem like this were all parents to accept certain rules as being true and right in raising their children. Since this is not the case, each parent does what seems to be right in his own eyes, or perhaps parents do what their children insist that other children are doing.

Frequently our search for truth ends too soon because of our failure to think through and measure and examine carefully those opinions and prejudices which are false but which try to get by as being the truth. Lots of people, for example, believe every word that they read in the newspapers, even though newspapers are constantly changing their stories and reporting different interpretations of the same event. Furthermore, most of us build up pictures in our minds of what we expect other people to be and this imaginary picture is what we regard to be true.

A young student, assigned to meet me at a station in Pennsylvania where I had gone to deliver a lecture at his school, revealed the common human mistakes of forming distorted images of others. He kept looking at every passenger, trying to guess which one might be the rabbi. Finally, when we were the only two left on the platform, I went up to him and introduced myself. Whereupon, he exclaimed, "But you can't possibly be a rabbi, for where is your beard?" On the surface, this is amusing, but it really is one of the tragedies of our life, for it reveals how easily and uncritically people come to accept as true whatever they may have picked up along the way of life with regard to strangers and other faiths and other groups. Most of us generalize to a point of sin. It is a statement of prejudice to say that all Yankees are like this, or Southerners are like that, or Frenchmen are this, or that all Germans are another thing. But we do this, and we say this, and we act upon it, and all the time that we do these things, truth is denied and prejudice and falsehood are affirmed.

It seems to me that the most commonly accepted test for the truth of anything is, does it work? We assume that

if it works, it must be true; and if it does not work, it is not
true. We moderns regard ourselves to be very practical
people and we glorify the practical and denounce the im-
practical. Thus, there are many people who hold the
United Nations in contempt because it has not as yet
worked and has not produced world peace. On the other
hand, vast multitudes acclaim the atom bomb and the hydrogen bomb and, indeed, all the armaments of war because
it is assumed that these will do the job, these will produce
results, these will knock out our enemies. Violence works,
we believe, so we are for it, whereas the ideal of peace
seems no more than a pretty dream and so we disregard
it.

I should like to stress very strongly here that essentially this "practical" approach to truth is immoral. It is
immoral because it is based upon the false principle that
the end justifies the means. Such a philosophy about truth
doesn't really care how you achieve your results providing
you attain your results. Thus, Communism resorts to every
device of tyranny and murder and violence and gross
deception in order to achieve the end—its objective, which
is the so-called classless society. The end justifies the means,
so go ahead and lie about the United States and vilify the
democracies and tell the struggling masses of the world
that America is the enemy of freedom-loving peoples.
Bore from within, use every possible means to bring about
the revolution to overthrow governments and to accomplish at last the victory of Communism over all.

Nazism, under Hitler, followed the same false principles
of Communism, that the end justifies the means—that anything is acceptable providing it works to get what you
want. Indeed, Hitler in his infamous autobiography, "My
Battle," urged the use of what he called the "big lie" and

boasted of the fact that the use of lies to gain your objective was highly desirable because it is very hard for truth to catch up with a lie and long before truth could overtake the lie, the Nazis would be in power. Believing that the end justifies the means, Hitler's Nazis brutally exterminated millions of innocent men, women and children and plunged our world into a ghastly war from which we have not yet recovered. Because so many people here and abroad have accepted as the test of truth that something must be true if it works, we have all been victimized by the cunning of power propaganda which seeks to capture, and usually does, the mind of man by every foul and dishonest method!

The practical approach is, at heart, immoral and cannot ever be the genuine test of truth. Now, certainly it can prove that something is a fact. For, alas, it is a fact that people can be propagandized into accepting the slogans of immoral leaders. We see the tragic consequences of this all around us. But just because something is a fact does not necessarily mean that it is also the truth.

Well then, what is the valid test of truth? It seems to me that the great philosopher Immanuel Kant gave us the best test of truth in something which he called the "categorical imperative." This distinguished philosopher said that we must act not from inclination but from duty and that a dutiful action derives its worth not from its consequences, but from some general principle. And what is this principle? Always to act in the manner in which we should wish all other people to act. And then, he went on to say: "To treat humanity, whether in thine own person or that of any other, in every case as an end withal, never as a means only."

All of us should be indebted to this great thinker, Kant, for his presentation of what is the very foundation of the structure of truth and moral behavior. It distinctly emphasizes the point that only that is true which has universal validity. It emphasizes the dignity of every individual and makes us realize that it is false and immoral to use any person as a means to an end. That is why the Declaration of Independence is such a mighty document, for it states, you will remember, "We hold these truths to be self-evident, that *all* men are created equal." Notice that it does not say that all Americans, or all the white race, or all the black race; indeed, it does not limit itself to any particular group—but it states categorically that *all* men are endowed by God with certain inalienable rights.

Recall, too, such statements from Holy Writ, as "Love thy neighbor as thyself"—"Thou shalt love the stranger as thyself"—"It hath been told thee, O man, what is good" —"Do unto others as you would have them do unto you" —"Man does not live by bread alone"—"Peace on earth, good will toward men"—there is no limitation in these immortal declarations of truth. Their reasoning and their teaching apply to every human being, no matter what his color, no matter what his creed.

Whatever thought you have which crowds out somebody else, which is limited, which is narrow, which is confined, which does not embrace all humanity, is basically false. The thought may be expedient, it may be a fact which works in your behalf, it may be something which is good for you or your group, but in the final analysis it is false because it is not universal in its application. Ask yourself, then, whenever you are about to embark upon any kind of behavior in relationship to your fellowman, ask yourself the question, "Would it be good for mankind if all the other people in the world were to do what I propose to do? What would happen to society if all were to do

exactly as I want to do?" Ask yourself also, before you act
or undertake to do anything with other people, with your
own children, your friends, your neighbors, your dear
ones, ask this question, "Am I just using somebody else to
get what I want—am I using other people as a means to
an end—am I respecting their own sacred rights—am I
respecting their dignity and status as a child of God?"

Moreover, I would like to add that another way to
know whether or not you are following the truth is to
examine your own attitude on any particular subject. If
your attitude is one of absolute, positive sureness that you
have the truth, if you are completely closed to any doubt
as to the veracity of your position, if you have become
stubborn about what you consider to be true, then I would
surmise that you are probably wrong. You should read
that profound part of the book, "Lost Horizons," by
James Hilton, in which the High Lama of Shangri-la tells
the Englishman, Conway, that he and his people of
Shangri-la believe in the laws of moderation. He tells Conway that he had discovered that moderation is true and
works in all situations. Then, when Conway exclaims how
wonderful it is to live by the law that moderation is true,
the High Priest softly says, "But, Conway, even with regard to this law, we are only moderately certain that it is
true." How wonderful this humility and modesty about
truth! Here there is no stubbornness, no obstinacy, no bigotry. In that episode, the author is advising you and me to
be humble, even in how sure we are about our highest
sanctities.

We should also take a lesson from the pure scientists
who are profoundly humble in their approach to truth,
for the genuine scientist always suspends judgment. He
is not absolutely positive. A Nobel Prize winner in science

disclosed this to me some years ago when we were discussing the humility of science. We had been talking about the procedures of science, the caution of science before it declares that anything is true—because in science for something to be true, it must be universally true at all times, under all conditions, and in every place. We came to mathematics and I said that at least we could take for granted that two times two was four everywhere, at every place, and every time. Then this great man said, "But the scientists, while accepting the truth that two times two is four, nevertheless concede that it is possible, under certain conditions, for two times two not to equal four."

What a better world this would be, how much more enjoyment of living there would be, if we were to approach the experiences of life using the method of the scientist which suspends judgment and the method of the philosopher which calls for surgical thinking, and the method of the great spiritual teachers which calls for universal application of all thought and conduct.

The great poet Schiller once said that if God came to him and spoke as follows: "Son of man, behold! in one hand I hold before you pure truth and in the other hand the search for truth. Now, choose which you will have and it shall be given to you." "I would say then," wrote Schiller, "that if God were to put such a choice before me I would reply, 'O Lord, pure truth is for Thee alone—give to me, I pray, the search for truth.'"

For you and for me, my friends, for every human being, this ought to be our golden choice. We are engaged upon the search for truth, a search which can never end. As Robert Browning put it so well, "A man's reach should exceed his grasp, or what's a Heaven for?"

Thus, our democracy, our beloved country's way of life

can never be finished—it must always be in the process of becoming—must everlastingly be reaching out and searching for higher and greater and better achievements. Likewise, in our attitude toward mankind, we should reject any doctrine of bigotry and prejudice which shuts out our fellow man, but rather we must venture further upon those paths which lead us into universal co-operation and world-wide concord. And in our own private lives, while being humbly aware of our own limitations, we ought to be confident that if we try to do those things which are based upon truths that are universal in their value and universally good in their results, we shall surely achieve contentment for ourselves and bring happiness to others.

CHAPTER XIV

The Problem of Criticism

THE SEARCH FOR TRUTH, as we have just noted, involves the use of our critical faculties. But we have not concerned ourselves with the more intimate applications of criticism to our personal lives.

For example, what happens when we criticize ourselves and our family? What about the consequences of passing judgment on our own deeds and upon the conduct of those around us? The following incident may shed some light on these questions. Some time ago, I sat in an office waiting to see a friend of mine. As I waited, I could not but over-hear part of a conversation which took place between two women in one of the adjoining rooms. Their voices were raised as they spoke and what I heard was this:

"Mary, I am the kind of girl who can take criticism. You may find fault with me, you may tell me that you don't like the style of clothes I wear or the kind of friends I have and I will still remain your friend." Whereupon, Mary replied, "I don't think that is possible. I think that if I were to start criticizing you like you say, that you would soon hate me." That is all of the conversation I heard because I then went in to see my friend, but I have not forgotten this observation on the subject of criticism. Surely the problem of criticism is constantly present in human relationships.

It seems to me that all of us are critics, whether or not we are qualified. The human being seems to be endowed with the irrepressible urge to declare about everything or anything either that he likes it or that he doesn't like it. No day can pass without eliciting from every one of us, whether frequently or infrequently, our applause and favor or our displeasure and disfavor. One cannot possibly live without exercising a choice between this or that commodity, or person, or ideal. We constantly criticize —whether we complain about the weather or talk about our favorite book. One cannot readily imagine horses or dogs or tigers or snakes meeting one another and expressing their likes or dislikes of their fellow creatures, of their food and the weather, outside, of course, of the realm of make-believe in fables.

To criticize, then, is a natural human characteristic. Moreover, in a democracy we are expected to be critical. We may go further and declare that in a free society, in a democracy where freedom and liberty are supreme virtues, the need for and the respect for criticism is essential to the normal and intellectual growth of the free society. Conversely, we may say that where criticism is stifled, where people are not allowed to say what they like and what they do not like, that there we have a slave state, a totalitarian state, a Nazi, a Fascist, a Communist state. Having recognized the natural human characteristic of being a critic and acknowledging its worth in our free society, I want to focus our attention, primarily, upon that aspect of criticism which applies to our relations with ourselves and with those around us.

The person who can be a good critic in evaluating himself is very likely to enjoy living. Constructive self-criticism enables you to choose the right from the wrong, the good from the bad. You know the best road to take to reach the goal you are after and you know what not to do and what not to choose. It means that you have sound judgment. It means that you know how to size up the situation and to act with intelligence upon a given subject matter.

On the other hand, to be a person of poor judgment means to invite disaster and failure and defeat at almost every turn. When you add to poor judgment the characteristic of being obstinate and stubborn, then you have a person who is bound to fail. I can't imagine a more devastating combination in any individual than to be afflicted with poor judgment and stubbornness at the same time. Such people are always making bad bargains and hugging them all the tighter, to their own and other people's misery. Often enough such unfortunate people keep blaming others for their troubles. If one is a poor critic, if one is a poor judge of things, then at least one should try not to be obstinate. Admit your mistake and try to do better next time.

But, did you ever try to get someone to admit that the mistake was his? Sometimes I think that the seven most difficult words in the English language to say are "It was my fault—I am sorry." Perhaps you are precisely this type of person who refuses to admit it when he is wrong. Whether you are or not, I am sure you will agree that a great deal of unnecessary suffering and trouble come into the world because of people who hate to own up to their own mistakes. This is painfully illustrated in traffic accidents. An experience of this kind happened to me some time ago. Some friends and I were sitting in my car, the last of a long line of cars waiting for a train to move past the crossing. While waiting we were busily engaged in conversation when, suddenly, we were jolted heavily from behind. I opened my door and came out of the car to speak with the man who had so unceremoniously bumped into us, when to my astonishment, but also I must confess to my infinite amusement, he shouted, "Hey there, wise guy, what's the idea of backing into me?" Very calmly I replied that I could not possibly have backed into him since I had turned off my engine while waiting for the train to pass. And then, before I could continue he exclaimed, "You are a liar, it's your fault." Well, fortunately no harm had been done to my car or to his, so I just returned to the driver's seat and that was that.

Now there you have an illustration of how some people will act in a situation which is of their own making. Almost automatically they will deny any responsibility. They will lie about it the way Adam and Eve did in the Garden of Eden when God accused them of eating of the forbidden fruit. Adam said, "The woman Thou gavest me, she made me eat it." And Eve said, "It is not my fault. The serpent made me eat it." Thus, according to the Bible, the very first man and woman manifested this reluctance to own up to our own mistakes. Surely world affairs would immediately take a turn for the better if we had the courage, when we are wrong, to say, "It is my fault, I did it, I am responsible!" But this is only one phase of the subject of self-criticism.

There is another side of self-criticism which is suicidal. There are people who are always finding fault with themselves, who can never see anything good in what they do, who are convinced that they were born for mistakes, for misfortune, for trouble. If anything, this is worse than the refusal to admit that one is wrong when one is really wrong. A person who looks upon himself as a hopeless misfit, who regards himself to be a failure and doomed to lose out in everything, will not only, alas, fail but also may deteriorate mentally and spiritually. You can sometimes see the first signs of this terrible personality defect when you either hear yourself say, or somebody else say, "I just know that I am not going to be able to succeed." The normal thing to say, of course, would be this, "I know the job isn't easy to do, but I am going to do my best in order to succeed." Instead of saying this, a person afflicted with destructive self-criticism makes up his mind, even before he meets with the challenge, that the problem is going to be too much for him.

For example, I have had young people come to see me all nervous about going away to college and meeting new people. They will say something like this, "Oh, I am sure that I am going to have a terrible time. No one will like me. I am going to fail in my subjects. I won't be asked to join a fraternity (or sorority). I will never be popular." To such a dark outlook, I try to bring whatever sunshine of confidence and hope that I possibly can, yet, even as I do so, I am filled with much apprehension for the future of these young people who have such a lowly estimate of themselves. On the other hand, a person should not be conceited, nor arrogant, but he should have a wholesome confidence and trust and faith in himself. Believe in yourself, have self-respect, aim for the stars, expect the best. You may not reach the stars, you may not achieve the best, but at least you will be striving for them and moving in the right direction.

Up to this point, we have discussed self-criticism. But what about criticizing others and receiving criticism from others? Perhaps the most dangerous kind of conversation is critical talk. There is, for example, the damage that parents often do, wittingly or not, when they criticize their children. I realize, of course, since I am a parent myself, how inevitable it is that conversation with our little children frequently is a matter of saying "don't do this" and "don't do that," or "that is not the way to do it, my child, do it this way—this is the right way." Furthermore, I know, as a parent, how aggravated one can become by the truculent and contrary behavior of one's children. Children can easily make you lose your temper and your control. Even so, after making due allowances for all the aggravation and irritation, there are some things that one should never say to a child, no matter how provoked one may be. One should never tell a child, "You are stupid, you are bad, you are impossible." Never say, "I hate you for doing this," or "You are hateful for doing that," or "Keep that up and you are going to end up in jail," or "There must be something wrong with you, you are just like your Uncle X or your Aunt Y—nothing good ever came of them, and nothing good is going to come of you." Shout such destructive criticism and dire predictions often enough to your child and you will most likely create a social misfit. Do you not see the tremendous difference between guiding a child constructively, helping him to see his mistakes in a spirit of love—and chastising a child both physically and verbally with violence? The one helps him to improve; the other destroys him.

One should never curse a child, never use profanity in criticizing a child. The same holds true between brothers and sisters, and husbands and wives. What a tragic household it is in which the people who make up the family curse one another, criticize one another ruthlessly, and are without mercy or kindness in their dealings with one another. In such a household, children and parents withdraw from one another and get a distorted view of life and of people in general. There can be no real happiness in such a household. There can only be pain and deep mental and spiritual hurt. Your home should be your sanctuary. Your home should be the place where you and everyone in it show love for one another, help one another, boost one another, cheer one another on. Why tear down your child, or your husband, or your wife, or brother or sister? They are your dear ones. They are your people, the closest to you in all the earth. You drive love away from yourself when you outrage those who are closest to you. Let others criticize your dear ones and, believe me, they will. People are much too ready, alas, to find fault. Don't think that anybody alive can escape criticism. But, at least your homelife should be free from that destructive fault-finding which deprives the persons in the home of a major source of much needed confidence and happiness.

Moreover, you should be very careful before you criticize your friends, before you find fault with people outside of your immediate family. Lord Chesterfield once said, "When a man seeks your advice, he generally wants your praise." Reflect upon that and you will agree. Most of us want to be told that we are right, not that we are wrong. When we go to our friends we seek approval, not disapproval. To be sure, there are times when a friend will ask you for advice, for your counsel, for your criticism. At such a time, you should be very careful about how you give it. Sugarcoat it as much as possible. Start off first by praising, show your love and appreciation for the noble side of your friend and then when you offer your judgment, when you must find fault, when you sincerely believe that your friend is about to do something, or is doing something, which is wrong, then cover your criticism generously with loving kindness.

There are enough sources for criticism in this world from

strangers, from others outside our family and beyond the realm of our close friendships, who think nothing at all of criticizing us and who do so—sometimes brutally. No one goes through this world without being savagely criticized at ·one time or another. When our children go to school they come up against criticism on the playground, they get criticized by their teachers, they get criticized by other boys and girls in all forms of play. When you go to work, you get criticized by the boss, or by your customers. From your neighbor to your preacher in the pulpit you are censured by any number of critics. Therefore, let your home be a place where, for the most part, your experience is one of loving approval, of a pat on the back, of helping you to go forward with confidence and with faith in yourself, in the work that you do. And when your friend comes to you, treat him softly and gently when you find fault, for from you he wants love and not criticism, even though he asks for criticism.

The Talmud has a very prudent saying which goes like this, "Do not judge, do not criticize your neighbor until you are in a position similar to his." Here, indeed, is a watchword, a measuring rod for all kinds of criticism. Here we actually get to the very heart of the matter, for it is when we have enough sympathy for another person, enough loving interest in somebody else, enough to imagine ourselves in his place, that we are acting like religious men and women, acting as civilized people should behave. You husbands and wives who bitterly criticize one another, please stop and think for a moment. Imagine yourself in a similar situation and what you might have done under those conditions. You parents who quickly spank your children, who find fault with them, who shout at them, who let your tempers loose upon them, please try to imagine yourself in the place of the little one who hasn't had your experience, who doesn't have your judgment, who is just beginning to grow up, who can so easily make mistakes. Put yourself in the position of your child before you criticize him. The same wisdom applies to all our human relationships, whether with our neighbors, whether with strangers, whether with peoples across the sea. Before you criticize a person, or the action of people, you must study the problem, think it through, use your mind, use your imagination, put yourself in the other fellow's place, and then you may offer your criticism for then it will be, I am sure, what we call constructive criticism.

There can be no denying, it seems to me, that constructive criticism helps the individual and the human race to make progress. We all need it—we are all the better for it. But, constructive criticism is based upon respect, upon love, and upon confidence. When you offer constructive criticism to somebody, you respect his abilities, you act in the spirit of loving kindness, and you have confidence in his future. This kind of criticism adds strength to the person criticized, and enables him to improve, to master his weakness and to attain his goal.

When we criticize one another, when we judge one another, let us be modest, thoughtful, and imaginative. Let us judge in kindness and helpfulness. According to the first chapter of Genesis, our Heavenly Father looked upon the earth and though He knew its imperfections, yet He called it "very good." He created man and though He knew man's weakness, yet, in His divine love, He called him "very good." And this was, and remains, the judgment of mercy, of love and of hope. Let this kind of criticism be the only kind in which we indulge. Let us be quicker to say "very good" than to say "very bad." When we must criticize adversely, and there are times when we should, let us do so in the spirit of compassion. When we must find fault, let us speak and act with sympathy and humility, and reverence for the sensitiveness and dignity and precious worth of every human being, remembering that we are more than flesh and blood, that each one of us is a soul —that each one of us is a child of God.

We have noted that all people of all ages are critical of themselves and others. However, older people tend to be much more so than the younger generation. As we age, we often become fixed in our thinking. We dislike change and are uncomfortable with new things. Hence, an old person can be constantly fussing about "what are they going to do next?" and "this younger generation is going to the dogs," and "when I was young," etc. Since the enjoyment of living is impossible for the bitter old-timer, let us consider the problem of how to grow old gracefully.

CHAPTER XV

Growing Old Gracefully

A YOUNG WOMAN recently exclaimed to me, "I hate to think of growing old. I want to be twenty-five forever." This cry for eternal youth is not rare. Most of us, if we have not joined in a similar outcry, have given some thought to the problem of age, of growing older. Surely it would be helpful to our enjoyment of living if we knew how to grow old gracefully. Here are several thoughts on this subject which may form a sound basis for such a constructive outlook.

First of all we had better recognize the obvious which is that age must come—unless, God forbid, we die young. Growing older is part of the experience of living, part of the cycle of existence. As long as we live we are involved in the process of getting on in years. When we are young we long to grow up and when we are older we often yearn to be younger. Now growing older can and should be a meaningful experience in maturation, in the deepening of understanding, in the widening of the horizons of knowledge. To rebel against growing older is stupid. Of course it is perfectly reasonable for a person to want to look youthful and to maintain an attractive appearance. However, it is wrong to become so obsessed with the "youthful" that one dresses entirely out of character. It is said that "there is no fool like an old fool" and there is no more effective illustration of an old fool than one who tries to act and look like a youngster.

If growing older is not regarded to be exactly a privilege it is due, for one thing, to the unfortunate fact that numerous opportunities are denied to people because of age. For example, we still have many jobs closed to people beyond forty-five and fifty. That age should prove such a handicap in our country seems ridiculous when our medical scientists and our health measures have increased the average age to sixty-seven, so that it will not be long before the majority of Americans will be in their fifties and sixties. Furthermore, there isn't a business enterprise in our country today which does not have to alter its rules with regard to age. For we have found that one cannot generalize and say that since a person has reached a certain age he is automatically disqualified from doing this or that. Some folks in their sixties are more vigorous than others in their twenties. Of course a younger man, on the average, will naturally have more physical vitality than the average older man.

But there are so many different things to be done in our world, jobs of infinite varieties, so many positions which require long experience and the wisdom of years, that it is preposterous to rule out any man or woman simply because he or she has attained a certain age. It is high time that we revise our thinking on age qualifications for positions, for we are living in a new world in which, through the miracles of modern medicine, through diet, through precautionary measures, we are able to live longer and remain stronger and fit and efficient far beyond any age that was even dreamed of fifty years ago.

The trouble is that we do not cultivate the attitude of respect for older people. We all need to renew our observance of the Biblical admonition to respect our elders. Now, I am not advocating an unreasonable worship of years in themselves. I am not insisting that just because a person is older than you are, that you must leave everything up to him, that his word must be the last word, that his wishes must be final on the subject. If we believe in the broadest application of the principles of Democracy, we must agree that the thoughts of young and old alike should be considered and everyone given his due. But it is a serious mistake on our part to allow ourselves to depart from those courtesies, those amenities of life which call for a respect for those who are our seniors in age. Young people should be taught to stand up when their elders enter the room. We ought to instill the discipline of loving kindness and tender consideration for those who are older than ourselves.

One may well lament the fact that much of the rich, warm quality of life is missing today because we do not instruct our children how to show the proper respect for their teachers, their preachers, their elders in experience and in age and in position. We have even gone through a period in which children call their parents by the parent's first name. This is not only a false standard of comradeship, but it also strikes me as being ridiculous. I think it is silly for a child to call his father by his first name and then to call the little boy he plays with by his first name, as if both were on an equal basis when they are not on equal terms. For your father is your father and your friend is your friend. With deep psychological insight, the Ten Commandments teach us to "Honor thy father and thy mother." Note that the word is "honor" which is to revere the position that your parent or your elder occupies in your life. No doubt there are some people who call their parents by their first name, who love them dearly and it works out beautifully. I don't deny that it can work out well in some cases but, as a general rule, I think it is wrong. I think it invites disrespect. I think that in time it tends to cheapen and degrade those relationships which are to be held sacred, because it rejects the discipline we can use to keep them sacred.

This whole modern fad of calling everybody "darling" and "sweetheart" and "pal," of debunking every tradition, of treating everybody from one's parents to the heads of our government without any reverence, without any respect, has tended to cheapen the dignity of life. Certainly it has contributed to our disregard for the aged, our failure to honor those who are our elders. Maybe one of the reasons why so many people dread growing older is because they see how pitiful is the lot of many who are older, how neglected they are, how shunted aside, how painfully rejected. People fear that they will be forsaken in their old age in a world where there is so little respect for the aged. Thank God that we still have some who have not permitted themselves to be swept aside by the modern fad of glorifying youth, some who have refused to be overcome by the insolent and destructive influence of disregarding elders. We still have a chance to recover for our society that dignified and noble standard of living which gives to people of every age, young and old alike, their proper position of responsibility and respect.

The importance of giving to every age group a position of dignity cannot be overemphasized. As we should honor age, so we should honor youth. As we should honor manhood and womanhood, so we should honor childhood. But we have not done these things. We have not equalized our approach to every phase of human existence. There were times when we abused childhood and it was necessary to pass child labor laws. There are times when we have neglected the needs of adolescents and the result has been a shocking amount of juvenile delinquency and breakdown in the observance of morals in our youth. But, constantly we have permitted old age, apart from old age security measures, to be a time of life which, in the majority of instances, has not been a satisfying experience. What I ask for the older people is no more than what I ask for human beings of any age. Nevertheless, I sincerely believe that if special honor should be paid to any age group, it should be to the older people because we should reverence life itself and show respect toward those who are the veterans of life's challenges, battles, triumphs and defeats.

But I would be presenting only a portion of the story about growing older gracefully if I did not deal also with the need for love which continues from the day of birth to the day of death in every human being. Most of us go along with the idea that the need to love and be loved belongs to young people. We have put romance into an age limit and believe that older people do not feel the need for romantic love because they have outgrown it and so they do not have the vaguest interest in romance.

It must have come as a tremendous shock to those who think thus, when the former Vice-President in his seventies married a charming and lovely widow, much younger in years. "Why, how is such a thing possible," many asked themselves. And many others said, "This is silly, he is just an old fool who must be slightly touched. Doesn't he know that he is over seventy?" That is how some people thought and spoke. But, the fool wasn't the former Vice-President. The fool was any person who talked injudiciously, for Mr. Barkley taught all of us the lesson, providing we were ready to learn, that romance and love defy all age limits. As long as we live we need one another, we are strengthened by love for one another, we find life a happier experience because of the comradeship and the devotion we feel one toward another. It seems as if God made the human being to thrive as long as he lives under the sunshine of love, even as he must wither away when love is denied. I believe it should be encouraging to all of us to know that there is never a time in our life, no matter how old we may become, when we stop loving, or stop needing to be loved. For what else brings us greater happiness than this bright blessing, this affection and love for one another? To love and be loved gives one a sense of being needed and fulfilling a need. And surely when you have that feeling that you are needed, you have the feeling that life is worthwhile, that there is a place for you under the sun.

To be sure, we are taught, when we are younger, to prepare in material terms for our old age. We prepare economically by the purchase of insurance policies and the establishment of pension funds. We have been taught to work hard in our youth so that when we are older we may be financially independent. This is very important and it is good that we are alerted to the economic needs of our later years. We should also be grateful that through our government we have moved in the direction of providing ourselves with some degree of old age security.

But we need more than money to be happy as we grow older. We need to love, to be loved. Furthermore, we also need intellectual and spiritual resources. We need to nourish our minds and souls. "Live and learn" should be our constant watchword. We need to educate our taste for good literature and art, for the enjoyment of pastimes like reading a good book, listening to good music, being able to indulge in interesting conversation. All these things we need so that as we grow older we can be spiritually secure and desirable to be with and to know. But the only way to do this is to begin when we are young. The enjoyment of art and music and literature is a lifetime enjoyment. These can fill our years with great happiness. These are an unfailing source of mental strength and part of our mature growth.

When we are younger the world expects from us energy and ambition. As we grow older, the world expects from us wisdom, counsel and the harvest of experience. But how shall a person have something to impart which is worthwhile if he has not enriched his mind through the years? Why should any one seek out an older person who is boring, uninteresting, and who has nothing important to contribute? You and I know older people who are sought out by others of all ages because they are truly stimulating as they discuss matters of importance. Who would not visit a person of mature experience for guidance and enlightenment? Indeed one might conclude if one is an older person and one is shunned by the younger generation, that it is the grim price we pay for our wasted years. It reveals that one has failed to make use of the opportunities in life to grow mentally and spiritually. When one is avoided, when one is passed by, when the younger members of your own family do not come to you, it is a sign either that you have been very selfish and have not cared for them, or that you are considered to be a bore, an impossible windbag whose latter years are filled with meaningless, inconsequential, narrow interests. Growing older gracefully is a matter of sharing with others the ripe harvest of the years. Just as in philanthropy it is a wonderful thing to give while you are alive, so in life in general it is good to give generously of yourself in every aspect of existence. But too many people are counting on the wills they leave behind, the legacies they bequeath, to fulfill their duties to the oncoming generation and not enough realize that we owe much more than an amount of money or a piece of property to those who come after us. Younger people need advice, they need ethical and spiritual guidance. The younger generation needs the wisdom which only people of experience can offer. Young people can be brilliant, but not necessarily wise. Deep wisdom belongs to those who have lived, who have matured with the years, who have learned from the school of experience. But the young seek out only the old who are lovable, who love generously, who rejoice to help the oncoming generation along the road of life and who really have something to say.

It is about time that we take heart from the findings of psychologists who assure us, on the basis of their scientific research, that we are never too old to learn. The history of the spirit triumphant over age is full of glowing examples of people who maintain a radiant mind and spirit until the day they die. I think of the distinguished Jurist, Oliver Wendell Holmes, who at the age of ninety sat down to continue his studies in Latin and Greek. I think of the Roman Cato who at eighty began the study of Greek. I think of the great Venetian, Titian, who at the age of ninety was still painting masterpieces, and getting better all the time as an artist; and writing to a friend that he, Titian, at the age of ninety, was beginning to understand what painting was all about. I think of Verdi, who at the age of eighty composed "Falstaff," which is considered by some critics to be his greatest musical work. I think, in our own time, of a man like Winston Churchill, whose youthful spirit, in his seventies, was undimmed as he led his nation once again as an inspiring Prime Minister. I think of Toscanini, who in his eighties was at the peak of his conducting career.

To be sure I have chosen some outstanding people, but the secret of their youthful spirit and genius is something that all of us should learn; for while we may not be the masters they are, we can at least learn from them where to seek the source of the young heart and mind. They teach us that all people who are aged, and yet remain youthful, are concerned with people, or interested in culture, or devoted to the enjoyment of enduring pleasures. There are, of course, exceptions but, by and large, you can remain young as long as you live by holding fast to your faith in life and in God.

Schiller once said, "Keep true to the dreams of thy youth." Here is another watchword to preserve the springtime of one's soul. Don't give way to skepticism and cynicism, no matter how difficult the road you travel. Say, rather, "Tomorrow will be better," "The best is yet to be."

A friend of mine, who is eighty-five, reminded me of a French proverb which goes like this: "Fifty is the old age of youth, and the youth of old age." Only a person who loves life can speak like this, only a person who refuses to let the clouds and the frustrations and the disillusionments of life overwhelm him.

George Santayana, a most eminent philosopher of the Western World, in 1942, at the age of seventy-nine, wrote the following: "Never have I enjoyed youth so thoroughly as I have in my old age. In writing 'Dialogues in Limbo,' and 'The Last Puritan,' I have drunk the pleasure of life more pure, more joyful, than it ever was when mingled with all the hidden anxieties and little annoyances of actual living. Nothing is inherently and invincibly young except spirit. And spirit can enter a human being perhaps better in the quiet of old age and dwell there more undisturbed than in the turmoil of adventure."

What a great pity it is that so many of us will not learn this lesson that age is a matter of mental and spiritual fatigue. It matters not how we make a living, how busy we are in the business of making a living, we all should take the time to help ourselves to remain young in our old age by cultivating spiritual, intellectual, and artistic pursuits.

How perfectly this is described by an anonymous writer in the following words which deserve to be repeated and memorized by all of us:

"Youth is not a time of life. It's a state of mind. It's a test of the will, a quality of imagination, a vigor of emotions, a predominance of courage over timidity, of the appetite for adventure over love of ease.

"Nobody grows old by merely living a number of years. People grow old only by deserting their ideals. Years wrinkle the skin, but to give up enthusiasm wrinkles the soul. Worry, doubt, self-distrust, fear and despair— these are the quick equivalents of the long, long years that bow the head and turn the growing spirit back to dust.

"Whether seventy or sixteen, there is, in every being's heart, the love of wonder, the sweet amazement of the stars, and the starlike things and thoughts, the undaunted challenge of events, the unfailing childlike appetite for 'What next?' "

"You are as young as your faith, as old as your doubt— as young as your self-confidence, as old as your fear—as young as your hope, as old as your despair.

"So long as your heart receives messages of beauty, cheer, courage, grandeur and power from the earth, from men, and from the Infinite, so long are you young.

"When all the wires are down, and all the central places of your heart are covered with the snows of pessimism and the ice of cynicism, then, and only then, are you grown old indeed—and may God have mercy on your soul."

Whenever I meet people in their late seventies and eighties, I ask them this question: "Tell me, judging from your experience, would you say that human nature is good, or do you think that human nature is evil? Tell me, do you think that life is worth living, or do you think it is in essence a tragedy?" I am happy to say that the overwhelming majority have replied that human nature is essentially good and life is very much worth living. But they have never failed to point out that life has to be *made* worth living. And as for human nature being good or evil, most of them believe that it depends upon what the individual does with his own capacities and what his environment has done to bring out that which is in him. One of them expressed it in these words: "Give a child love and understanding and with very few exceptions, he will become a fine human being. Show him hate, reject him, deny him, and he will develop into an unhappy, miserable person, a source of trouble everywhere." But just as interesting as are the wise observations of these older people, is their background, their own personal history. They themselves are the living witness of what I have tried to state here, which is that with loving parents, with dear ones who really care, with minds that are alive and constantly enriching themselves, with a firm trust and faith in God, all of us can grow older gracefully. And even if we be denied some of these blessed influences, we can by our own resolve make life as we grow older a maturing experience which finds us rejoicing in every day by contributing to the happiness of all those who are around us. The secret of growing older gracefully seems to be a matter of giving—the giving of one's best, wanting to help, of desiring to make life a happier experience for others. It is a question of unselfishness. It is a problem of wanting so much more to give than to receive.

Perhaps we should use the word "adulthood" as Dr. Harry Overstreet advises, instead of such words as "old age." For what is childhood and youth but a preparation for adulthood! We should consider adulthood as unique in meaning and opportunity. It is that time of life when we can put to use the wisdom we have obtained in the adventure of growing up. It is a time of life which should justify all the labor and sacrifice and learning we have experienced as we mount the ladder of the years. Once we look upon being older as the crowning climax of the maturing process, we can understand and accept the glorious truth of Robert Browning's poem in which he wrote:

"Grow old along with me, the best is yet to be—the last of life for which the first was made: Our times are in His hand, who saith, 'A whole I planned,' youth shows but half: trust God; see all, nor be afraid."

CHAPTER XVI

Meeting the Unexpected

ONE DAY a wise old man said something to me that I have never forgotten. He was talking about the need we all have for courage to meet the tribulations which come to each of us at some time or other. And he said this:

"One of the greatest human problems is how to meet the unexpected."

He went on to say, "Most of us do pretty well in our efforts to handle those trials and challenges which we know are coming, but it is an altogether different story when the unexpected befalls us, for when the unexpected happens, most of us are unprepared." I have often pondered on these remarks, and the longer I have lived, the more I have come to see the soundness of his observation.

The majority of us do get along fairly well within the normal range of those testing experiences in life to which the human being must adjust himself. If a man knows that he is going to need an operation, he will arrange his affairs accordingly. He will manage to see to it that he has the right surgeon, that the time will be convenient and that his business or professional duties will be covered during his absence. But what a different thing it is when the operation is an emergency, when he is struck down suddenly as in an accident. Then he and his family are taken unawares and it requires a tremendous amount of spiritual and physical capacity to meet this unexpected blow.

Again, consider the illustration of a person who is working at a job, making his living, when he realizes that a change must be made for his own welfare. He then proceeds as best he can to rearrange his life, to seek out and find some other position so that he is not stricken economically and can handle his obligations and meet his responsibilities adequately. But what a tragic story it is when unemployment strikes a man unexpectedly, when he loses his job suddenly, when he finds himself without means of support or is bankrupt overnight. The great depression of 1929 is still fresh enough in our memories and the long lines of unemployed a vivid enough picture in our minds to make us appreciate what havoc came into the lives of millions of people in that era of economic tribulation. We can recall the numbers of suicides, the broken homes, the misery which overwhelmed so many people. As much as anything else it was the unexpectedness of the disaster, the lightning swiftness of the crushing change which caught millions of us unprepared and, therefore, was so destructive. The facts of life support the validity of my old friend's comment that the most trying blow comes not from the expected but from the unexpected crisis.

Since this is true, what about modern man's preoccupation with the idea of security? A major concern of the human being today, as we have noted in previous chapters, is to be secure—to have a security which, he hopes and believes, will cover all the eventualities, all the incidents and contingencies of his life. And so we speak of the right of every man to a job and the right of every person to medical care and the right of every person to a safe old age.

We live in a time when we speak of security from the cradle to the grave and our assumption is that by being prepared economically, having sufficient money, we shall be secure as long as we live, no matter what happens. What is most surprising about this passion for economic security is that we should worship it so much and rely upon it so completely when we are living through a period in which over and over again the power of money has vanished, has been broken, has been rendered meaningless in the face of unexpected national and international tragedies. For what did money mean to the Germans following World War One? What does money mean to most of the people in the world today?

To be sure, some currency, some economic system, is used to facilitate the numerous relationships of the individual with society. But the threat of war and the task of preparing for war make money the most vacillating, the most changing, the most unreliable factor when we are looking for help when the unexpected trial comes upon us. We have seen in the United States what war does to our economy and we are faced with even greater problems, titanic in nature, as we look ahead and seek to find the ways and means to prepare ourselves for life in a world where our philosophy of life clashes with an opposing philosophy. Yet, long before the modern world's crazy cataclysmic changes in which monarchies have been overturned, in which money standards have been overturned, the history of mankind has given us ample evidence of the folly of placing one's hope upon financial security as the most reliable means of meeting the unexpected.

Money knows no master except that it masters those who have it. Money brings many things, many conveniences, many luxuries, much power, but it does not necessarily bring contentment, nor can it guarantee in and of itself that stamina to endure. In our society we need economic security. We need material sustenance. But for anyone to cherish the belief that economic security is invincible is to reveal a childish appraisal of life, a naive faith which will be shattered when hurled against the harsh rocks of the unexpected realities.

If it is not economic security that is regarded as man's unfailing support, then it is likely to be scientific development, or intellectual progress, or mental capacity which is held to be the secret of meeting successfully whatever comes. We have come to accept as a matter of course the slogan that through science and through education we shall solve life's problems. Obviously, we need to further scientific progress and to favor the growth of education. Whoever would stand in the way of science and mental development is as foolish as the man who would attempt to hold back the tides of the ocean. Indeed, it is thrilling to mark the advance man has made in scientific achievement during the past century. We have revolutionized the world, that is, the world of "things." We can move swiftly from one place to another. We can send our voice around the world. We have extended the life span. We have radio and television. We have automobiles and telephones and airplanes. We know how to move under the seas and how to dig tunnels under mountains. Science has made the modern world a fairyland of inventions which enthralls us and which excites our imaginations as to the further conquests which may be made in the future.

We live in a time when more of us go to school than ever before, more of us read, more of us understand the phenomena of nature. We have more museums, more music, more libraries. The very atmosphere in which we live is an atmosphere of learning, of becoming informed. And it is good that we should live in a world like this. No one wants to go back to the Dark Ages. No one wants to return to an era of ignorance and superstition and obscurantism. We want to develop our minds. We want to be able to think clearly. We wish to continue our pursuit of knowledge and truth.

And yet, science and education and the pursuit of knowledge are evidently not enough to meet the unexpected. Let me remind you that of the many appalling facts which came to light in World War Two, none was so stark as this, namely, that out of the fifteen million men called to arms at that time in our country, three million were judged to be unfit because of mental disturbance. Many among these three million were brilliant boys, possessors of high degrees acquired at notable colleges and universities. There was nothing wrong with their studies or their learning, but they could not meet the unexpected blow of being thrust into war.

Moreover, there is no surety that scientific and mental prowess make for peaceful relationship and harmonious contacts with others. The students of philosophy will remember that the first subject that Plato taught in his Academy in ancient Athens was music, because he indulged the hope that when knowledge is first based upon the appreciation of harmony, its end result would be harmonious living. But Plato had not been dead a decade when Alexander the Great thrust Greece and the whole then-known world into war. And scarcely twenty-five years passed when the whole Mediterranean world was plunged into the darkest moods of pessimism and despair.

But we need not go as far back as ancient Greece to see that education is not enough to guarantee harmonious liv-

ing. Look at Germany in our time. The Germany prior to
Hitler was one of the most educated countries in the
world. It was the country of Bach and Beethoven and
Brahms—the country of Goethe, the country to which
students from all over the world went to receive the most
coveted higher degrees in education from such universities
as Heidelberg and Berlin. But all this education availed
nothing in the crisis. When a situation arose which chal-
lenged the soul of Germany, she drove the world into a
terrible war which is still upon us and whose end no man
can yet foresee. Education is important. It is fundamental
in the life of our world and certainly in the life of a democracy, but it is folly to believe that education by itself is
enough to prepare us for the unexpected and to enable us
to endure. To you and to me, as individuals, education is
a requisite, a basic requirement for knowing how to do
things, for gaining insight and understanding into the secret of the cosmos. But in the day of the whirlwind and
the hour of the storm, we are defenseless if all we have is
knowledge.

Well, then, if money isn't the secret to meeting the unexpected, and knowledge, education, is not the sure road
to courage in the face of sudden change, what is it that
provides us with the power to meet fearlessly whatever
comes? I find the answer in the following episode from
the book entitled "So Little Time" by John Marquand.
The leading character, Jeffrey Wilson, is haunted by the
sorrow that has come to so many parents in our day, the
sorrow of seeing a child go off to war. He is overwhelmed
by the realization that we allow so little time in our lives
these days for the development of those values in human
relationships and for the understanding of those ideals
which all of us need in order to live courageously in an

era of worldwide upheaval. The following scene is at the very end of the book. Jeffrey, after saying good-by to his son, walks up Fifth Avenue in New York regretting that he has had so little time to know his son, to be with him, to show him his love. Almost before he knew it, the boy had grown to manhood and now the unexpected blow of another war had come and his son was in the army. He thinks about the ephemeral nature of life, the swift changes, the rapidity with which time passes, our involvement in those things which have only superficial importance, when his eyes fall upon St. Patrick's Cathedral and he walks into the great church.

And there, at last, in the quiet and dimness of the sanctuary, he becomes aware of the only reality which abides though all things change, the only power which is timeless, which is eternal. All at once, this parent, whose entire life has been engrossed in the business of making a living, in being busy with innumerable details which had no permanent significance, recognizes that he has overlooked the one force in the universe which can lend meaning and power to our brief sojourn on this earth—Jeffrey Wilson recognizes God. Long ago the Prophet Zechariah said, "Not by might and not by power, but by my spirit, saith the Lord."

I have come back to the old, old story, the ancient faith, the ideal that faith in God is the only unfailing source of inner fortitude if we would possess the capacity to meet the unexpected and to prevail over it. You will say that I am prejudiced and that because I am a rabbi and a religionist, I am only advocating the theories of my own profession. But I beg of you to believe that this is too glib a cancellation of the validity of my position. The evidence of history is on my side. The logic of life supports me.

Consider—what other means is there to enable us to confront triumphantly the startling, bristling events of our lives with abiding equanimity and fortitude, with enduring trust and courage? We need the faith of the psalmist who said, "God is our refuge and strength, a very present help in trouble. Therefore, will we not fear, though the earth do change, and though the mountains be moved into the heart of the seas. . . ." (Psalm 46) To be able to meet the unexpected with the strength everlasting you must be able to say, and to mean it with all of your heart and soul, "I believe in God."

CHAPTER XVII

"Death Came as a Friend"

THE TRAGEDY OF DEATH when understood and graciously accepted is truly the richest soil in which the mind and soul of man can grow in strength and beauty. For sorrow, when accepted with faith and courage, can be a matchless artist. Then he is able to use the soul for his canvas and tears for his paint.

In the deepest darkness of our grief, in the blackest night of our bereavement, sorrow can find the light by which to work. He does not inform us of his progress. He never tells us when the picture is finished. We know what he has done only through some sudden strength which we possess, in a new meaning we have found in life, in the enrichment of our spiritual power. Sometimes he reaches up out of the heart to touch the face and afterward there is a serenity and soulful beauty in the eyes and countenance which was never there before. For sorrow, when we let him, can be an artist of such unlimited creative scope that he can transform any one of us into a finer, better, nobler human being.

Unfortunately, not many of us let sorrow be an artist. We don't want to think about death. We run away from it. Even at a gathering of friends, before and after the funeral, it is rare to hear any mention made of the deceased. People seem to have joined a conspiracy of silence toward death. When you visit the mourners you may discuss any subject you choose with the exception of the departed. Very often the minister is advised not to deliver a eulogy nor to go beyond reciting a few psalms.

Moreover, the deceased is dressed up in the coffin as if he is about to attend a formal dinner party; he simply must be made to appear like anything else except the fact that he is dead. The funeral director knows he has "satisfied" when he hears the people say of the deceased, "He looks so natural." And by the way, please notice that we seldom use the word "undertaker," because that is too brutally frank, too clearly linked with burial. Much better to call him "funeral director," or better still "mortician."

Furthermore, we keep the children away from funerals. We don't want to depress them. Let us tell them rather, "Your daddy has gone away," or "Your mother is on a distant journey." Apparently our slogan is "Don't mention the word 'death,' don't think of it, forget it." This is the modern attempt to run away from the most profound and inevitable fact of every living thing.

It is time that we stopped playing this silly game of self-deception, because we are upsetting innumerable lives. There are too many nervous breakdowns and mental breakdowns because of our refusal to face the fact of death. It is high time that we faced up to the inevitable sorrows of life, for in the long run trying to escape from reality is harmful. Our attitude toward death should be as normal and natural as is our attitude toward birth. For birth and death are part of the experience of each one of us, and both demand faith and courage.

Not that I am asking for a constant preoccupation with the subject of death. A thousand times no! The Chinese say, "You cannot prevent the birds of sorrow from flying over your head, but you can keep them from nesting in your hair." Agreed! However, it is a great mistake to shut your eyes in order not to see the "birds of sorrow." They are there. We must deal with them.

Fifty years ago, people in general believed in immortality. A minister knew, when he stood before his congregation, that immortality was a cardinal doctrine accepted by his flock. Today, however, many people do not seem to believe as their fathers did—in immortality. There is the feeling that death is the end. Modern science, which began by breaking with the belief in the presence of a spiritual force in the universe, but which has since gone a long way toward accepting the reality of the spirit, is still a major influence in making people's attitude toward death one of complete rejection of the theory of immortality.

A large part of the materialistic goals of our time—the passion for living *now*—the modern version of "eat, drink and be merry, for tomorrow we die"—that sort of thing is rooted in this attitude that death is the end. A quality of hardness and coldness comes into our lives when death is seen as the final chapter in the human drama.

There are many, however, to whom death is a mystery. They have not made up their minds about it. They are not convinced that death is the end, but neither are they convinced that there is any evidence for immortality. These people realize that despite dismissing death as the final word on life, the human heart does not let go when it truly loves. There is such a thing as grief and sorrow and mourning for one who has gone. To find solace, they recognize that more is needed than to be told, "Oh well, just be strong, buck up, be brave, your loved one is gone but try to make the best of it."

For when we really love somebody, we cannot say good-by just like that. The beloved dead are not like possessions which are discarded when they are broken. Thus, there is something which agitates those who cannot make up their minds about death. Obviously, there is the end of the physical presence, but just as clearly the loved one continues to live on in the hearts and the memories of those who loved him. These people are repelled by the cold, negative conclusions of those to whom death is the end, but they are afraid to come nearer to the warmth and the light of those faithful, to whom death is the beginning. In this dilemma they are very unhappy, as any person must be when caught between two choices which are so far apart in consequence. Frequently a mourner cries out to me, "Oh, if I could only believe in immortality! What a comfort it would be to me—how it would strengthen me. I need to believe in it so much, but I just can't get myself to accept it."

How fortunate, indeed, are those who have come to accept the belief that death is but the gateway to immortal life. With Tennyson they are able to say:

"Twilight and evening bell,
  And after that the dark,
  And may there be no sadness of farewell
  When I embark;
  For though from out our borne of time and place
  The flood may bear me far
  I hope to see my Pilot face to face
  When I have crossed the bar."

Or with the Psalmist of old, they can exclaim, "I shall dwell in the house of the Lord forever." (Psalm 23) Such people come to their death like Socrates whose heroic end is described by Plato. Socrates, we are reminded by Plato, was condemned to death because he believed in freedom of the mind. His friends were weeping as they stood near him in his prison cell. He asked them to hold back their tears. He could have escaped but he was willing to accept the punishment—to drink the hemlock, that poisonous drink which would bring on death. Socrates told his friends of his faith in immortality and then he closed his eyes with faith and resignation because he believed that death was but transition—death was a beginning. He loved life intensely, enjoyed it greatly, but he was unafraid of death.

These valiant spirits who face death with the assurance that it is not the end are a diminishing number among so-called "enlightened" moderns. Yet, behind all of the modern man's rejection of immortality, he still feels the hunger and the yearnings for the solace which comes only from such a belief. For man cannot escape from his essential nature. He is more than flesh and bone. He is higher than the animal. Yes, he recognizes his own limitations, but he also senses his infinite potentialities. And that is why it is so important for us today, in a time of such universal discontent and sorrow, to understand that we are immortal.

For upon what *death* means to the living rests the basis of what *life* means to the living. If death be the end and we become convinced of it, our entire approach to life changes. For then we are only the creatures of the hour, a moment's foam on the crest of the wave of life, a glimmer of light in the eternal darkness, a spasm of energy before oblivion. But if we see ourselves as children of eternal life, then is our experience on this earth imbued with high meaning and responsibilities. We are part of destiny. We are already eternal. We belong to the immortal realities. We have obligations, duties to perform, and we are as eternal as the God who created us is eternal. It is only then that we can say with the Psalmist, "The Lord preserveth all them that love Him." (Psalm 145) It is only then that we can look out upon this vast universe and instead of feeling our littleness and insignificance, be moved to exclaim with Biblical fervor, "I shall not die, but live, and declare the works of the Lord." (Psalm 118)

The awareness of the tragic in life ought not to be destructive. It does not have to lead us to pessimism and morbid renunciation. On the contrary, it should quicken us to a vivid awareness of the constructive meaning of death. To remember, always, that each one of us must some day depart should open our hearts to the ennobling impulses of love and loyalty. For once we appreciate fully the implication of the fact that life for us, as individuals on this planet, does not go on forever we ought to become kind and sympathetic and humble. Yes, humble. For what is our power and greatness, we whose days pass away like a shadow? One by one we drift into the mystery of the night of silence. One by one we leave to depart on that journey which takes us into eternity. How then can we deal cruelly with one another, how can we neglect and disappoint our loved ones, how can we be harsh and indifferent? But we do these terrible things to one another much too often. And the reason why we are capable of such reprehensible conduct is because we forget, or refuse to realize, that someday death will come; and so we give no thought to its meaning.

Another frightful result of our refusal to think about the meaning of death is to be overwhelmed by vain and foolish regrets when death takes a loved one from us. Of course there are justifiable regrets. We may have many reasons for being conscience-stricken over what we have done to our dear ones while they lived. Alas for the son or daughter, the husband or wife, the parent or friend, who did not measure up to the demands of a situation, who were tried and found wanting. Alas for those who showed hatred and not love, base ingratitude and enmity instead of tender thoughtfulness and affection. Theirs is a pitiful plight from which it is not easy to recover. The only healing for them is to repent sincerely. The only redemption from such bitter regret and remorse is to devote oneself to a life of unselfishness, of loving service to others.

But these justifiable regrets are entirely different from the vain and foolish regrets which assail so many loving and devoted people after a loved one dies. Yet a mourner obsessed with foolish regrets can suffer as much from remorse as the person who has cause to feel guilty. For example, I have often heard a mourner exclaim, "Why didn't I do more for my dear one? Why did I cause him so much trouble in the way I argued and differed with him?" Or, "He might still be living if I had only called in another doctor, taken him to another hospital, been with him when he was stricken."

Such regrets are vain and foolish, and should be forgotten. If you are a mourner you should not chastise yourself because you and your departed dear one quarreled or argued or differed at times. All human relationships are subject to moments and sometimes days of disappointment and disillusionment. The Bible tells us of the many occasions on which the children of Israel failed their leader Moses and caused him to cry out in despair against their stubbornness. The devoted disciples of Jesus abandoned him in the hour of his greatest need. And yet, the children of Israel went on to honor and love the teaching of Moses, even as the disciples of Jesus continued to teach the message of the Nazarene to the world. You must realize that misunderstandings will take place and do take place in all families, in every human experience. Why should you remember the few occasions when you were at odds with your dear one and forget the larger part of your relationship, which overflowed with happiness and love and peace? When you do this you are unfair to the memory of the departed, because your loved one would want you to find joy and inspiration in your recollections.

Similarly, it is vain regret to dwell upon what you might have done to prolong the life of your loved one if you had called in this or that consultant, or had been able to go to some other medical institution. In these days, our doctors are given excellent training and leave no stone unturned as they carry on their sacred mission of conquering disease. Modern hospitals in cities and towns have high standards and the patient, with rare exceptions, is given the best of care that medical science knows.

I should like to add a word here about those well-meaning friends who come in, after someone dies, and then upset the mourners by insinuating that another doctor or another hospital might have done better. When we come to comfort mourners, let us bring solace instead of pouring salt upon the wounds of grief by adding vain regrets.

However, the more we think about regret following the passing of a loved one, the more we understand that the very nature of a loving relationship makes regret inevitable. To quote from a beautiful passage of a memorial prayer in the book of prayers of Reform Judaism: "The sorrow of separation is the inevitable price of days and years of precious love; tears are the tender tribute of yearning affection for those who have passed away but cannot be forgotten." Since this is true, all of us should realize that a day will come when we are going to feel desolate because of the sorrow of separation. This should teach us to show love and devotion to one another while we live so that when death comes to a dear one we shall not have cause to be ashamed of what we have done. If you have drifted apart from your family because of misunderstandings, now is the time to heal the breech. Oh, how bitter are regrets when you gaze upon the lifeless form of a dear one and you know it is too late to make amends. Oh, how tragic are the regrets for not having acted in love while there was yet time and the opportunity to do so.

Some years ago I heard of a remarkable man who was undaunted by affliction and magnificent in his understanding of the meaning of death. Let me tell you about him.

To the Memorial Hospital in New York, during the last weeks of summer, they brought the dying physician, scientist and poet, Dr. Hans Zinssner. He was a man of superb humanitarian achievement; his life was devoted to the mastery of bacteriology and dreadful epidemic diseases. For seventeen years he had been professor of bacteriology and immunology at Harvard Medical School. At the summer's end he died, surrounded by his wife and son and daughter and a few devoted friends. One of the beautiful legacies he left behind was a poem he had written some time back, which appeared in his autobiography entitled, "As I Remember Him." Read this poem, this proud and gentle outpouring of the heart's deeper wisdom:

"Now is death merciful. He calls me hence
Gently, with friendly soothing of my fears
Of ugly age and feeble impotence
And cruel disintegration of slow years.

Then he concludes with these wonderful lines:

How good that ere the winter comes, I die!
Then, ageless, in your heart I'll come to rest
Serene and proud, as when you loved me best."

It is everlastingly true—a blessed truth—that in our hearts our loved ones never die. Thus are we given the power to make them immortal for us. Death may part, but love builds a bridge between the seen and the unseen. To know and to understand this is to master the meaning of tragedy and to be triumphant over death itself.

However, the noblest tribute to our beloved dead is to make their precious memory the greatest inspiration for consecrated living. It is not enough to cling to their memory in our hearts. It is even harmful to our own peace of mind and destiny to mourn the loss of dear ones in prayers and tears alone. We must go forward in the spirit of the patriarch Abraham who, so the Bible tells us, came to the grave of his wife Sarah, wept and then rose to meet life. He did not shut himself off from life in the bleak solitude of sorrow. The poet Mary Lee Hall presents this thought in her poem "Solace," in these words:

"If I should die and leave you here a while,
Be not like others, sore undone, who keep
Long vigil by the silent dust and weep.
For my sake turn again to life and smile,
Nerving thy heart and trembling hand to do
That which will comfort other souls than thine:
Complete these dear unfinished tasks of mine,
And I, perchance, may therein comfort you."

Indeed there is greatest solace to be derived from completing the "dear unfinished tasks." To carry on in someone else's memory, to do something which is noble and to be able to say to oneself, "How pleased would my dear father be if he knew of this"; to bring happiness to others and to say, "How my beloved mother would rejoice," is to find true consolation. In precisely that moment our loved ones are alive again. It is when we remember, when we direct our lives in accordance with the ideals our loved ones have given us that there is no death, that there is only the unbroken line of spiritual life.

All this, thus far, is a philosophical attitude toward death which is taught by religion, to be sure, but which any intelligent approach to life embraces. Judaism and Christianity, however, go one great step further. These religions teach us, though the body is dust and returns to dust, the spirit returns to God who gave it. The immortality of the soul is one of the great convictions of our faith, which rises logically out of a faith in God. Our God is a God of love, who never fails to place that answer in the universe which satisfied a fundamental need of our bodies and cry of our hearts. We have thirst and there is water to quench it. Hunger and there is food. The longing for comradeship and there is love and friendship. The quest for truth, and the world yields its great secrets and laws to the patient and inquiring mind. Yes, and there is this yearning for immortality. And God will answer that yearning. How He does it, we do not know, but that we live on with Him has been, and is, the unchanging conviction of some of the greatest intellects throughout the long history of mankind.

I refer to intellects and spirits like Isaiah, Jeremiah, Plato, Aristotle, great rabbis and saints and priests, great thinkers like Spinoza and Kant, great modern minds like Milikan, Compton, William James. All these giants of the mind have, more or less, come to the same conclusion, that the universe is essentially spiritual, that our world is much more than surface appearance, more than materialism, physical matter; that this universe is dynamic with purpose and meaning, that the universe is full of that glory which we religionists call God.

On the death of King George VI, Mr. Churchill delivered a beautiful eulogy, saying, among other memorable things, "During these last months, the King walked with death as if death were a companion, an acquaintance whom he recognized and did not fear. In the end, death came as a friend, and after a happy day of sunshine and sport, after 'good night' to those who loved him best, he fell asleep, as every man and woman who strives to fear God and nothing else in the world may hope to do."

I, for one, am drawn irresistibly to the words in this quotation which read, "death came as a friend," for I believe it is true. The peace that comes to the face of each one of us when we die, reveals the touch of a friend. The relief from the infirmities of age, the surcease from pain and illness, from the suffering and miseries of a host of afflictions which torment this weak flesh of ours, all these pass away like a cloud under the benign, friendly touch of death.

Yet, infinitely more important than this peace which comes after the storms and struggles of life are over is the function of death, the friend, as it opens the portals to eternal life. Thus, while life is high adventure, death is the supreme adventure before which the people of faith do not cringe. When the moment comes to depart, they are like Columbus setting out on a journey over a dark and unknown sea. Before them stretches the vastness of the deep, strange and awesome. Yet they are unafraid, for the light burns in their souls, the light of faith, of the sure knowledge that across the dark waters of the unknown is a harbor, a tranquil destination—God!

Oh, let us deal kindly with one another, for we are all pilgrims along the same road which leads, at last, to the same end. Yet, conscious as we are of the limitations of the years, let us also be joyously aware of the unlimited horizons of the spiritual life. With gratitude in our hearts for the life and the love of dear ones and with unfaltering trust in the God we love, in whom there is no death, let us go forward on our journey upon this earth, brave and undaunted—companioned by our exalted memories—strengthened and sustained by the mighty faith that the spirit of man is immortal—that when death comes to us, as he must to every living being, he will come to us as a friend—a friend who tenderly and gently leads us to our eternal home.

CHAPTER XVIII

The Greatness of Man

DR. KARL MENNINGER, the great psychiatrist, has said: "Attitudes are more important than facts."

This statement is profoundly true. The happiest children I have ever known were a group of blind children whom I had the privilege of teaching for several years in New York City. No matter how depressed I might have been before I came to this class, my spirits were always uplifted by being with these handicapped youngsters. They were full of smiles, gentleness and laughter.

I have also seen happiness among old people in old folks' homes. I have found contentment among those who are hopelessly ill. I have found courage in those who are apparently defeated. I have been profoundly moved by the humble resignation and the undaunted spirit of people who have lost their beloved.

To be sure, I have seen the opposite—I have seen despair and fear and disillusionment and the breakdown of the human spirit. But most people are inspiring in their capacity to rise up after they have been overthrown—to continue their journey when they have been detoured by misfortune. Yes, we can be proud of the human race. We can rejoice that we are human beings. We shall eventually build upon this earth a society which shall fulfill the dream of the Prophet who described the golden age saying, "And the knowledge of God shall fill the earth as the waters cover the seas." (Isaiah, 11:9)

The background against which I write in praise of the human being seems to contradict my affirmation. We are threatened by an even greater war than the tragedy we have known in World War Two. We are living in an age of suspicion and distrust and plotting and war preparedness. Atom Bombs and Hydrogen Bombs, deadlier planes and violent death, occupy the headlines of our newspapers. The atmosphere we breathe is charged with the electricity of tension and crisis. The skies of our civilization, today, are filled with the ominous piling up of storm clouds which threaten the security and freedom of all mankind once their colossal energy is unleashed in the hurricanes and cyclones of destruction.

And still I say, "It is a good thing to be alive, it is a privilege to be a member of the human race and I profoundly believe that at last we shall leave the lowlands of sorrow and enter the highlands of universal peace and happiness." Why am I so sanguine? Why is my optimism so certain, and my confidence so sure? It is because I find in the human being the qualities of greatness which come from his faith and love, from his idealism and sacrifice.

The faith of human beings, the world over, is truly wonderful to behold. The ancient historian, Plutarch, once said, "You may find communities without comforts, without skills, without kings and no need for these things; but a community without gods, without some spirit that they worship, no man has found, nor ever will find." This universal belief in a supreme power is the most remarkable evidence of the unique greatness of the human being. Religions may differ in theology and doctrine; they have different scriptures, traditions, and customs, and rituals.

But at heart they are the same. They are the manifestations of man's awareness of God.

In the sacred writings of the Hindu religion, I came upon this sentence which I think is beautiful, and true:

"The different faiths of mankind are like so many pearls in a necklace, and God runs through all of them like the string."

This vivid image of the necklace of faith, which stresses the essential harmony of the human aspiration toward God, must never be forgotten. It reminds us that though there are many religions, the wonderful thing to realize is that men do have faith; and though there are many forms of art and culture, the fact at which to marvel is that the human being yearns after truth and beauty. Granted, that there are times when men will deny God, as, for example, in Russia today, where under the monolithic leadership of the Kremlin, atheism is proclaimed. But, where is there a man, no matter how learned, no matter how vast his knowledge of history, sociology and anthropology—where is the authority or the prophet who would declare that this frigid decision of the Communist hierarchy will stand unaltered forever?

On the contrary! All the facts of human nature assure us that the people of Russia will, some day, cast out their cruel masters, as once they threw off the bondage of the Czars. The attempt of the Kremlin to murder the soul of the Russian people cannot succeed—it is doomed to failure because the human being will not tolerate indefinitely such a contradiction of his basic nature. Nor in our own country, where materialism and secularism seem so powerful, will we fail to see, eventually, a repudiation of the false gods, and a wholehearted return to the one true God. For deep are the roots, my friends, deep are the roots of the soul of man and though he may stray and wander and for a time depart from righteousness, yet will the soul refuse to be uprooted and ultimately come unto its own. For as the earth holds a tree, so God holds you and me. Deep are the roots of our faith and vast is the earth and powerful is God and He will not let us go.

I am reminded of that supreme prophet, Jeremiah, whenever I think of those who would no longer have faith in God. There was a time when Jeremiah became depressed in spirit and he feared that he could no longer hold fast to God. But it proved to be impossible to escape. In the twentieth chapter of the writings of Jeremiah, we read: "O Lord, Thou hast enticed me, and I was enticed; Thou hast overcome me and hast prevailed; and if I say, 'I will not make mention of Him nor speak any more in His name,' then, art Thou become as a raging fire within my heart; I strive to withstand it but I cannot." (Jer. 20:7) The eloquence of Jeremiah reveals how impossible it is for the human race to run away, permanently, from faith in God. As the writer of Psalm 139 put it, 'Whither shall I go from Thy spirit? Or whither shall I flee from Thy presence? If I ascend up into heaven, Thou art there; if I make my bed in the netherworld, behold, Thou art there. If I take the wings of the morning, and dwell in the uttermost parts of the sea; even there would Thy hand lead me, and Thy right hand would hold me. And if I say: 'Surely the darkness shall envelop me, and the light about me shall be night'; even the darkness is not too dark for Thee, but the night shineth as the day; the darkness is even as the light."

Not only is the faith of man great, but also his love. To quote from the Song of Songs, Chapter 8, verses 6 and 7:

"Set me as a seal upon Thy heart, as a seal upon Thine

arm; for love is strong as death; the flashes thereof are flashes of fire, a very flame of the Lord. Many waters cannot quench love, neither can the floods drown it; if a man would give all the substance of his house for love, he would utterly be contemned."

The moment one pauses to think about the human capacity to love, that very moment one becomes conscious of the divinity within every human being. As there are many kinds of flowers, so are there many kinds of love. There is the love between man and woman. There is the love between parents and children. The love of country, the love of truth, the love of justice, the love of humanity. There is the love of nature, of art, of science, of music, of literature. Get a human being to love something, and there is no obstacle too hard for him to master in order to reach his beloved. Love surmounts all barriers. It laughs in the face of danger. It is supreme in its confidence. It is proud in its devotion. A human being is the captive of love, and never is a prisoner so happy as when he is imprisoned by the bonds of love. If you want to see a human being happy, then you must see a person who is in love. Would you find a person who regards this earth to be a paradise and this world to be Heaven itself? Then find one who is in love. Life begins when we are in love. Life is fulfilled when we are in love.

"I am my beloved's and my beloved is mine," cries the lover of the Song of Songs. Listen to Ruth, as she pleads in accents of love with her mother-in-law, Naomi: "And Ruth said, 'Entreat me not to leave thee, and to return from following after thee; for wither thou goest, I will go; and where thou lodgest, I will lodge; thy people shall be my people and thy God my God; where thou diest, will I die, and there will I be buried. The Lord do so to me, and more also, if aught but death part thee and me.' " (Ruth 1:16)

It is because I can never forget the love of my sainted father for his wife and his children; the love of my great teachers for their disciples; the love of patriots for their country; the love of my wife and my children; the love of friends; and the love of those who can never stop bringing happiness to others, that I refuse to surrender my pride in being a member of the human race. And that is why I am certain, as you must be certain as you remember love in your own life, that mankind will endure and enter at last into an age of universal brotherhood.

Of faith and love I have written, but I could not do justice to the greatness of the human being without also praising man's recognition of ideals and his capacity for self-sacrifice in behalf of these ideals. Upon a sandy beach of the Gulf of Mexico, near my city, sat a young man one afternoon. He loved life as much as you and I do. He was as zealous to preserve his life as anyone could be. He had as much for which to live and to love, as you or I. But, out of the nearby waters came the cry of two girls for help! Two girls who had been swept out by a vicious undertow. And when that cry for help reached the ears of this young man, he arose and went to their rescue and brought them into safe waters. But, in saving them, he had expended his own strength and thus sacrificed his own life for others whom he had never known.

Why will we not remember this beautiful act of sacrifice and keep recalling over and over again the acts of selfishness we encounter? Why will we conclude, after reading in our papers about a murder, a robbery, about the evils in life, that these reports represent the true picture of the nature of man, when the truth is that only a few are guilty. The glorious truth is that the majority of the human race is decent and kind and honest and loving. It doesn't make any difference what the color of our skin, what the nationality, what the language, what the religion —everywhere you find God's children, everywhere you meet the thrilling evidence of the greatness of humanity.

This proud, affirmative celebration of life and mankind, of confidence in the future, however, must be protected and fortified by a courageous, fearless and intelligent acceptance of life's inevitable troubles. For sorrow, in some degree, comes to all. Hence, without this protection and deeper insight, the art of the enjoyment of living can seldom be mastered, nor pride in the human race be long maintained.

I remember a young couple, with whom I met to discuss their wedding ceremony, who made the following request of me:

"We don't know whether we are stepping on your toes or not, but do you have to say in the ceremony such things as 'do you promise to love one another in health and sickness, in prosperity and adversity, in good and evil days, 'til death do you part?' We don't see why you must bring into our ceremony even the vaguest suggestion of 'death' and 'sickness' and 'evil days' and 'adversity.' Just keep it happy, Doc, keep it pleasant. We don't want to be reminded of the clouds in life."

Such an attitude is not unusual. Many people try to make believe that there are no clouds and that all is sunshine. But, what is most remarkable about this tenacious clinging to a carefree optimism is that it is indulged in the presence of the most glaring facts which ought to moderate, if not eliminate, our unbridled, utopian expectations. The most superficial contact with reality should make it obvious that you cannot have everything. You can have much, you can perhaps attain a great part of your dream, you can experience a thrilling moment, a brilliant achievement, but it is a temporary victory. As someone put it so well: "Life gives us but moments, and for those moments we give our lives." But, beyond these moments, beyond these mountain peaks of achievement, there are the long and low valleys of waiting, of working hard without receiving reward, of the monotonous, futile pursuit of the pot of gold at the end of the rainbow. Very often, the valley of drudgery is by far the larger part of our mature experience. In those cases where we are able to enjoy the uplands of fulfillment more than we suffer the lowlands of despair and disappointment, we are singularly and uniquely blessed. I do not know of one aspect of human experience which goes contrary to what I have said here. Whether it be marriage or parenthood or friendship or childhood or adulthood; whether it be as citizens of our beloved country, as workers in any cause; whether it be in our business or professional lives, the fact remains that you cannot have everything.

Much of the current despair over the ability of the United Nations to establish world peace is due to our past unrealistic optimism. You cannot expect everything from the United Nations to take place within a short time. It is unrealistic to believe that in a world which is so different in many of its aspects, with civilizations running counter to one another, with freedom here and tyranny there, with plenty here and starvation there, with education here and illiteracy there, that it is possible with all of these diversities, with thousands of years of a history of violence behind us, to achieve in one or two years, or ten or twenty, a world covered with peace as the waters cover the seas.

How much more intelligent it would be, how much more realistic, how much better it would be for all of us, if we guarded our optimism with a healthy portion of realism. Then we could keep our hopes and dreams for world peace despite the set-backs, despite the differences, despite the outburst of hostilities within the United Nations' discussions. With this healthy realism, we would remember that "Rome wasn't built in a day," that peace takes a long time to come into being, that you don't change the world overnight. Our minds could then be calm and steadfast, instead of upset and disturbed and enraged. We would then not be so ready to rush to extremes, as we are now. Knowing that the attainment of peace is a difficult and lengthy process, we would hold on, when the going is rough, to our fondest dream for the coming of a day when men would "beat their swords into plowshares and their spears into pruning hooks."

How wise, how profoundly brilliant, were the prophets of the Bible who predicted the coming of a Golden Age, but who said it would take place "at the end of days." It was a long view, the realistic view. They knew that it takes time to build a world of brotherhood, of international justice and universal peace. But we, alas, are impatient. We want to get things done speedily. We can't see any reason for dilly-dallying, for waiting. "Let's get the job done in a hurry," is our motto, and if it doesn't get done in a hurry, then it is a bad job and we had better have nothing to do with it. I cannot emphasize enough the importance of forsaking this childish attitude and adopting the mature attitude which recognizes that you cannot awaken the brave new world until it is ready.

We need the same patience in our family life, in our personal life. Don't expect your marriage to flow smoothly all the time. Don't expect your children to be perfect always, your friends never to fail you and your job, your position, your profession never to fill you with disappointment and despair. You have to work at these things patiently and expect much disillusionment.

We are all human beings and since we are human and not divine, we are prone to make mistakes, to make errors. We are human and so we become ill, we become enervated. At times, our temper may get the better of us, our wisdom may not always be wise enough. We are human and so we are all a little bit weak, a little bit afraid and given to compulsions and superstitions. For there are nights when we are restless with uncertainties and cannot sleep and days when we are worried. We are captives of time, caught between the mysteries of birth and the mysteries of death. We lose, sometimes, that faith in God which alone can rescue us out of our captivity. We become burdened by the sense of our mortality. For we are mortal and not divine. We are human and not angels. For every laugh there is a tear, for every cry of joy there is a cry of sorrow, for every song of victory there is a lament of defeat.

Now this realistic appraisal of life—remembering that you can't have everything and usually get very little of what you deeply desire—by no means is to be construed as a sad and melancholy view of our existence. Actually, the world, as we experience it, can be our highest good and our greatest happiness just because of its limitations. Were we to have everything, were all our dreams to be fulfilled and all our expectations realized, there would be a monotony in life that would make it intolerable. I like the way Henry van Dyke expresses this point in his challenging poem "If All The Skies":

"If all the skies were sunshine,
    Our faces would be fain
To feel once more upon them
    The cooling splash of rain.

"If all the world were music
    Our hearts would often long
For one sweet strain of silence,
    To break the endless song.

"If life were always merry,
    Our souls would seek relief,
And rest from weary laughter
    In the quiet arms of grief."

There is a keen Oriental proverb which goes like this: "All sunshine makes a desert." This poem and proverb and the philosophy they express are not an excuse, not a covering-up, for the tragic side of life. I think they speak the truth and give us strength. I think that they go deep into the understanding of the real nature of our lives. Mature people are made not out of good times but out of bad times. Man's extremity is God's opportunity. It is in a crisis that the best in us comes to the fore. This very age in which we live, which is so turbulent, so confusing, so uncertain, is an anvil upon which God can remake us for the good, for the better. It is in the encircling gloom that we come to realize the importance of being led by the kindly light of the Eternal One. It is in the night that we can see the stars which are invisible by day. What I am asking for is mature outlook, reasonable expectations, a calm and steadfast mind and the patience with which to meet whatever comes with courage and faith in God, instead of with bitterness and resentment.

Now, if you were to ask me something like this: "Granted, that a person cannot have everything, any more than a nation can have everything, what really remains in which to believe? What can a person have? Give me something positive which will enable me to master the art of the enjoyment of living, come what may. I know that I am in the valley of disappointment and despair a good deal of my lifetime; I often doubt that there is anything at all in which to believe. What kind of creed would you advocate for life in a world like ours?" And here is my answer:

First and above everything else, *believe in God*. Even though your prayers go unanswered; even though your fondest hopes and dreams are unfulfilled, believe in God. For this belief transforms you from an animal into a human being, from a creature of flesh and blood into a soul. One of the scholars of the Middle Ages once said, "I believe just because it is absurd." While this, at first, sounds like a shocking statement, yet it is very profound.

Certainly it seems to be absurd to believe in a God of Love in a world of so much hate, in a God of peace when the world is so full of war, in a God of justice when there is so much widespread injustice. Nevertheless, its absurdity comes about only because of the contrast between a perfect God and imperfect man. We must hold on to our God-belief in order to rescue ourselves from utter hopelessness. Your belief in God is your claim to dignity. Your belief in God is your dream of a better world that shall yet come into being some day. Your belief in God makes you "but little lower than the angels" instead of companion to the beasts. Your belief in God is your light in the darkness, your pillar of fire to guide you through the night in which you are lost, your pillar of cloud to lead you aright in your day and in your time of trouble.

And then you must *believe in yourself*. You must believe that you are of precious worth and endowed with infinite capacity for the doing of good, for the discovery and the speaking of truth, for the making and the appreciation of beauty, for the wonder and the glory of loving and being loved. The day you lose respect for yourself, you lose your soul and you are a slave. The day that you stop believing in yourself, you will lose the confidence and the love of others. Each one of us is a mixture of good and evil, of strength and weakness. Thus it is easy to think poorly of one's self, to be afflicted with guilt-feelings, and to be downcast by a conscience stricken with regrets. Because of these guilt-feelings and these regrets, we become as nothing in our own eyes and as a consequence, lose our morale for life.

Believe in yourself. Stop the useless and futile waste of your courage and strength by indulging in vain regrets and by the blaming of yourself for some wrong that you did, or imagined that you did in a spiritual sense, to yourself and to others. Once you have made your repentance, once you have acknowledged the wrong and made amends to the best of your ability, if there be a wrong, do not go back to it over and over again, fondling and playing with your worries and fears and guilts as though they were some toy. Forget it! Be grateful that you are *you* and envy no other person! Believe completely in yourself!

And then you must *believe in mankind*. This, perhaps, will be the hardest of all to do, but you must do it. You must do it the way Job said he believed in God. Job said, "Even though He slay me, yet will I trust in Him." This is precisely how you must believe in mankind. Even though men slay one another, though they assault one another in wars, and curse one another by their hatreds, and disillusion one another by their greed and vanity, by their consuming selfishness, nevertheless, you must believe in mankind. Never surrender your faith in the human race, your belief in the coming, some day, of a generation better than any other of which we have ever dreamed. Mankind, by the grace of God, has come a long way in the past six thousand years of recorded history, but we have a much longer way to go and the happy goal is not yet in sight. Mankind today still presents the disturbing picture of a world which in the main is hungry and poverty stricken and sick.

But we have moved upward. We have begun to conquer the easy things first. We have learned how to move faster, to communicate faster. We are even learning how to prolong life, to overcome diseases. Yes, we have learned to fly in the air like birds, and to swim in the waters like fish—we have invented and use great airplanes and submarines. But we have not learned to live on earth like the sons and daughters of God. Yet this is, after all, the final triumph, the last and the best victory. We must keep on believing in a mankind that has discovered God, that has written noble scriptures, that already possesses a pantheon of saints and martyrs who died for the sanctification of God and for the rights of man! We must believe that a mankind which already has a Magna Charta, a Bible, a Declaration of Independence, a Constitution of the United States of America, a Bill of Rights—that this mankind is on the right road and some day will reach its divinely ordained destiny of universal peace and happiness.

And last, but by no means least, I would say that you must *believe*, and you can believe, *in freedom*. Freedom is your life and your length of days. Freedom is the difference between life and death for you. A slave lives a shadowy, a phantom existence, a slave is in bondage, a slave is afraid. But you must abhor slavery and love freedom. You must love freedom so much that you will resist any person or any movement that threatens your freedom. To-day, because of the threat of oppressive Communism, which is the classic example of the slave state, we who are the classic example of the free state find ourselves, paradoxically enough, in an atmosphere of suspicion and distrust which has been fomented by some well-meaning but misguided patriots who, in the name of preserving American freedom, are actually destroying it.

Let us reject any man or group who endangers the sur-vival of our religious, academic and political, our eco-nomic and social, freedom. With all that we are and yearn to be we must believe in our country. Believe in her not in the spirit of chauvinism, not in the sense of "my country, right or wrong, my country." Believe in the United States of America because she is indeed the "land of the free and the home of the brave," a country which, with God's help, we shall always keep "a government of the people, by the people and for the people." Believe in America as the hope of all mankind and so live your life that we shall become worthy of bringing humanity a bit closer to the dawn of the Golden Age.

Lift up your head and be proud that you are a human being. No matter what happens, don't lose faith in the hu-man race, nor in yourself. The jungles tried to destroy us and we survived. The tyranny of thousands of years tried to crush our faith and love and yearning for freedom, but all these violent attempts have been in vain. Slowly, pain-fully, sacrificially, proudly, the human race has come up from the jungle, from slavery, from feudalism, into wars and out of wars—sometimes slipping back, but not all the way back—onward and upward, fighting and struggling to be free.

For what is there to fear when we believe in the eternal power of God, the eternal truth of love, and the everlasting presence of idealism and self-sacrifice within the human mind and heart!

You can't have everything in this life, but you can, through believing in God and in yourself and in mankind and in freedom, come into a world of the mind and the spirit which is satisfying, which despite the storms and troubles of life can provide you with a fortress within, a mental world in which you do have everything that really counts for the real enjoyment of living—your faith, your courage, your undying love, your wisdom, your appreciation of beauty, your inner peace.